DERF
TALES O_ ...
AND MURDER

David Bell

COUNTRYSIDE BOOKS
Newbury, Berkshire

COUNTRYSIDE BOOKS
3 Catherine Road
Newbury, Berkshire

To view our complete range of books,
please visit us at
www.countrysidebooks.co.uk

ISBN 1 85306 813 6

Designed by Mon Mohan
Typeset by Textype, Cambridge
Produced through MRM Associates Ltd., Reading
Printed by J. W. Arrowsmith Ltd., Bristol

Contents

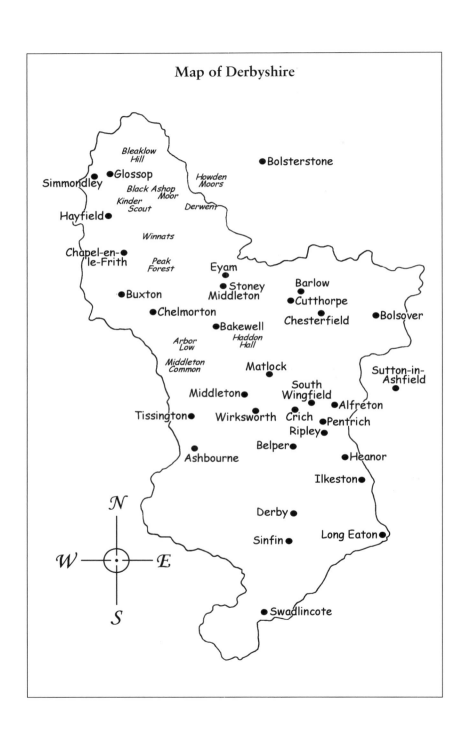

Map of Derbyshire

Introduction

The eleven chapters of this book include a number of murder cases, including the Bakewell murder of Wendy Sewell in 1973. A seventeen year old youth, Stephen Downing, was charged and served twenty-seven years for the crime but was then released and his conviction ruled unsafe. In another astonishing case, Flo Siddons and her family struggled for eighteen years to get a Derby man convicted for the murder of her grand-daughter Lynn. The authorities were finally forced to take action after a civil action where Flo successfully sued the guilty man and his stepson for damages resulting from the crime. Another case dates from Glossop in the 1920s when Albert Burrows killed his common-law wife and her two children, throwing their bodies down an airshaft of Simmondley Pit. He escaped detection initially, but was apprehended after he committed another child murder three years later.

Mysterious doings in high places are the subject of two of the stories. In 1817, a number of Derbyshire men were put to death – by hanging *and* posthumous beheading – for organising a rebellion against the government. It was not long, however, before government *agents provocateurs* were found to have been behind the whole incident. Similarly, exactly a hundred years later, a Derby woman was charged with conspiracy to murder, and incredibly her alleged victim was the Prime Minister, David Lloyd George. Although she was found guilty and sentenced to prison, it was later established that she was framed by shadowy government agents who objected to her activities in helping conscientious objectors and deserters to escape.

There is, too, a chapter dealing with a time when Derbyshire proved less welcoming than today towards visitors, regarding them with suspicion and even killing them. Other chapters look at Derbyshire's many pagan legacies, which perhaps owe their continued existence to the claim that more people of

Celtic descent live in Derbyshire than anywhere else in the Midlands.

Several ghosts – a surprising number of them Scottish – make an appearance, as do the mysterious voices of the ramblers who took part in the Kinder Scout mass trespass of 1932. Other mysteries include a number of Derbyshire witches, the appearance of phantom wartime aeroplanes seen flying over the high moorland of the Dark Peak, and a visit to the strangely powerful stone circle at Arbor Low.

David Bell

Acknowledgements

I would like to express my grateful thanks to David and Jean Moorley of Kniveton, Dr David Clarke, the staff of Swadlincote library and Derby Local Studies library, Peggy Davies and Sue Hickinson at Glossop Heritage Centre, Glossop Tourist Information Centre, Gemma and Carol of the photographic department of the *Derby Telegraph*, and Dave Ashton of the Upper Derwent Information Centre.

STRANGERS
AND COUSINS

———————————— ❀ ————————————

Derbyshire is not a county of high population, though it does have Sheffield and Manchester just outside its borders. It is not surprising therefore that thousands of visitors come to enjoy its beauty every day. All of them are made welcome, whether they are daytrippers in Matlock Bath or seasoned ramblers on Kinder Scout.

But it was not always so. There was a time when a stranger was looked on with suspicion, a possible source of danger. And a possible source of ill-gotten gains for those who were not averse to violent crime. These strangers did not need to be from outside Derbyshire, they could just as easily be from a town ten miles away or a village just up the road. As in the rest of the country, Derbyshire people could be extremely parochial. Parents would want their daughters to marry a young man from their own village – 'people like us' – not one of those odd people from the village five miles away.

In the 1750s, two strangers rode into Castleton. Their names were Alan and Clara and they were runaway lovers. Clara's family did not approve of the match because, although Alan came of a good family, he was not rich enough to make a suitable husband for her. The young couple decide to elope, and were heading for Peak Forest where the local priest was able to conduct marriages without parents' consent. Peak Forest was the Gretna Green of its day.

In Castleton, Alan and Clara stopped for a rest in a local inn where they were observed by a boisterous quartet of local miners drinking in the bar. The men quietened down and listened as the landlord gave the couple directions, advising them to head down Winnats Pass, a rocky ravine a mile or so along the road. The miners noticed the good clothes that the strangers were wearing, and speculated that they might be carrying a large amount of money. When the couple went into another room to eat a meal, the four young miners resumed their drinking, getting so rowdy that the landlord eventually threw them out.

The men decided to wait for the young lovers to set out again on their journey and planned to rob them then. They picked up a fifth man, armed themselves with pickaxe handles and headed for Winnats Pass. There they waited, until they saw their victims riding into the rocky ravine. They leapt out and pulled the man and girl from their horses, which quickly bolted back towards Castleton. The men roughly searched Alan and Clara, and shouted with delight when they discovered they were carrying £200.

The terrified couple were pushed into a barn, while the locals discussed what they could do with this newly acquired fortune of £40 each. When the men re-entered the barn, Alan begged them to spare their lives, but the men just stared silently at him. Realising that the men could not and would not show any mercy, Alan hurled himself at them. His reward was to be clubbed to death. Clara watched in horror as her lover died, and then suffered the same fate. The men looked at the two dead bodies, and decided to dispose of them down a disused local mine shaft.

When the riderless horses bolted back to Castleton, it was realised that the young couple had perished, but the exact method of their death was not known. The murderers did not enjoy their new wealth. A year after the murders, John Bradshaw met an early death, being killed by falling rocks, and Nicholas Cook died when he fell from a buttress. Both of these accidents occurred in Winnats Pass, which raises issues of ironic justice and the possibility of the very rocks themselves wreaking revenge on the guilty men. Tom Hall and Frank Butler found the knowledge of what they had done too much to bear, the former committing suicide and the latter going insane. The fifth man – Jim Ashton – used his share of the loot to go into the horse trading business, but all his horses fell ill and died. It was Ashton who left a deathbed confession to the strangers' murder, naming the others as his partners.

The skeletons of the murdered lovers were discovered ten years after the crime. The saddle from Clara's horse can be seen on display in the little museum at Speedwell Cavern.

Another stranger who met an untimely death was a Scottish pedlar who used to go through the north Derbyshire villages selling trinkets, lace and ribbons. One of his best weeks was always at Eyam Wakes, but one year he had competition from a number of local men who decided to sell trinkets themselves. The Scottish pedlar reported them for peddling without a licence, and the neighbourhood constable stopped them from trading.

The Scotsman had a good week, but his local rivals were angry at being reported. They were 'after his blood' and followed him to Stoney Middleton. The landlord of the Bull's Head in Eyam knew the men meant the pedlar harm, and sent a burly manservant to accompany the man to Stoney Middleton. Once the pedlar had entered the Moon Inn, the bodyguard returned to Eyam. In the Moon Inn, the resentful locals pretended friendship with the Scotsman, and joined him in a game of cards. During the game they accused their victim of cheating and dragged him outside. The pedlar was never seen again, but his skeleton – identified by its buckled shoes – was found later in a nearby cave known as the Carl's Wark. Another stranger had found Derbyshire less than welcoming!

The man who caused death and misery to Sir Hugo de Burdett and his wife Johanne in the Middle Ages was not a complete stranger, though he did come from forty miles away. Hugo and Johanne lived in a castle at Knowle Hills near Ingleby, close to the River Trent. Sir Hugo was very content with his life there. He had everything he could possibly want, a fine home, good lands, and a beautiful young bride whom he loved. Then the villain of the story turned up to visit him. He was Baron Boyville from Castleton, and he was Hugo's cousin. Boyville was pleasant and charming to Sir Hugo on the surface, but underneath he was measuring up the land and castle, which he coveted. As for Lady Johanne, Baron Boyville took one look at his cousin's young wife and was overwhelmed with lust. If anything were to happen to Hugo, then the castle, the estate and above all the lovely Johanne would be his for the taking.

Soon after his cousin had returned north, Sir Hugo was visited by a wandering friar named Bernard, who began to talk about the Crusades. It was the duty of every nobleman to go to the Holy Land, he informed Hugo, to fight the infidels. Sir Hugo was not interested; he had everything he wanted here in Knowle Hills. But, as the friar went on and on, Hugo agreed very reluctantly that it was probably his Christian duty to help to rescue the Holy Land. He would have to leave Derbyshire and venture abroad. With great sadness, he told Johanne that he was leaving for the Crusades. His bride wept and pleaded, but in vain. Hugo swore that he would be back in five years, and asked her to be faithful while he was away.

During her husband's absence, Johanne spent her time embroidering an altar cloth, using her own hair as well as gold and silver thread. She also scratched the words FIVE YEARS on a locket which she wore around her neck.

After a couple of the five years had elapsed, Johanne had a visit from Baron Boyville. He had terrible news, he told her, though he seemed unable to keep a smirk from his face. The bad news was that he had heard that Hugo had been killed in battle. As the heartbroken girl wept, he attempted to cheer her up by informing her that she should not mourn because he – Baron Boyville – was willing to make her his wife.

Johanne was having none of it, and informed her eager suitor that she would not even consider remarriage until the five years were up. Gritting his teeth, Boyville decided that she was worth waiting for, though he continued to visit the castle and to press her to marry him.

When the five years were almost up, Johanne reluctantly agreed that she would marry Baron Boyville. He was extremely delighted at this turn of events, and was walking round what was soon to become his new estates when he had a shock. There marching over the hillside was his cousin, Sir Hugo, back from the Crusades, eager to reclaim his Derbyshire lands and his young wife. Baron Boyville thought rapidly, then told his cousin that it was good to see him home! However, he continued, it was a bit of a waste of time, since he and Johanne had been lovers since the time Hugo had left. Boyville described their quite fictitious amorous activities in salacious detail, and Sir Hugo drew his two handed fighting axe. Boyville drew his heavy sword. There was only one way for the two men to settle this and combat commenced.

The battle lasted some time, but because Sir Hugo was in better fighting shape he eventually slew his villainous cousin. At this stage the story sounds a happy one: the villain is dead and the hero is back. But, as Hugo left the dead Boyville lying on the ground, and walked back to the castle, the lies that he had heard began to prey on his mind. It was probably true, he decided, that while he had been enduring the hardships of the Crusades, Johanne had been unfaithful with his cousin.

In fury he entered the castle, and when his wife saw him and rushed joyfully towards him, her arms held out in welcome, he cut off her hands. Without speaking, he strode off leaving the bewildered and heart-broken girl to bleed to death.

After Johanne's funeral – which he did not attend – Hugo became a bitter recluse, sending all but one retainer away. He refused all visitors, and closed up most of the rooms of the castle, eating and sleeping in just one. Years went by, then decades. He was an old man when one day his servant informed him that a dying hermit living in a sandstone cave by the river wanted to see him. Although Hugo had not left the castle in all the years since his return from the Crusades, something told him that it was necessary to go and see this hermit.

Alone he walked down to the cave, known locally as Anchor Church, and spoke to the hermit, who looked vaguely familiar. The man told him that he was the Friar Bernard who had persuaded him to go to the Holy Land all those years earlier. To the horror of Sir Hugo, the man then went on to explain that he had been bribed to do so by

The cave known as Anchor Church near Ingleby. (Derby Local Studies Library)

Baron Boyville of Castleton who had designs on Sir Hugo's lands and wife. Hugo now realised that the wife he had slain in jealousy and rage was an innocent victim of his cousin's plot. It is not recorded whether Hugo was able to grant forgiveness to the hermit for his part in the intrigue.

Hugo returned to the castle and began to open up all the rooms. In Johanne's chamber he wept when he found the locket with the words FIVE YEARS engraved on it. The altar cloth embroidered with his wife's hair was later given to a nearby abbey. Sir Hugo now knew for certain that his wife had remained faithful to him, but it is doubtful whether this knowledge brought him any satisfaction or happiness. The killing he had committed on his return from the wars in the Holy Land was now starkly revealed as what it was: a pointless act of jealous barbaric cruelty.

THE PAGAN
LEGACY

———————— ❖ ————————

Down the centuries, Christianity and the older Celtic religion of paganism have vied for the minds and hearts of people, and in Derbyshire the struggle seems to have lasted longer than elsewhere.

In the churchyard in Bakewell is a fascinating example of Derbyshire's dual nature. It is a sixth century stone cross, with on one side a carving of the Christian crucifixion, and on the other pagan symbols of the Norse gods Odin and Loki. Presumably the family of the man buried beneath it was hedging its bets! What it does show is that in that period paganism and Christianity existed side by side.

At other times, the Christian authorities tried to put down the older religion. In the 7th century, the Archbishop of Canterbury banned dances or rituals that involved 'the putting on the head or horns of beasts, for this is devilish'. Thus the pagan gods sacred to the Celtic people became devils in the eyes of the Christian church. Later, Christianity became more subtle in its attempts to supplant the pagan tradition. Many churches were built on pagan holy sites. Over the Staffordshire border in Abbots Bromley, the reindeer horns worn by the dancers of the ancient Horn Dance are now kept in the village church for 364 days of the year, only emerging for one day every September to be used for their original purpose.

In Derbyshire, the prime example of how the newer religion took over the practices of the older is found in the tradition of well-dressing. Although a few villages in Staffordshire and Nottinghamshire have adopted the idea, well-dressing has its roots in Derbyshire. Every year, some sixty-five Derbyshire villages take part, many of them decorating several wells. The first well-dressing of the year takes place in early May, and the last in mid-September.

Once known as well-flowering, the craft consists of decorating wells and springs with pictures made from flowers, moss, leaves and seeds. Even wool and eggshells have been used. The objects are pressed into clay beds in wooden frames, frequently a main frame measuring perhaps six feet by four, and sometimes flanked by two side panels. The materials used are always natural substances, usually growing things. Woe betide the village that experiments by allowing the use of non-acceptable materials to creep in. Neighbouring villages will be quick to condemn the non-conformists, and long-standing feuds have been known to result.

The villagers of Barlow, Cutthorpe and Wirksworth were always extremely careful to follow the unwritten rules. In 1948, one man who had been dressing wells for forty years wrote to the local paper to condemn two 'so-called well-dressings' in Buxton. 'Had such wells been erected in Wirksworth,' the indignant writer thundered, 'the committee and inhabitants would have been drummed out of town. Very little of natural growth other than dog daises and bark were used. Our competitors would be suspended if they used one ounce of anything not naturally grown.' The writer concluded by inviting the Buxton committee to come to see the genuine Wirksworth well-dressings, saying that if they did so 'they will be disgusted with their own feeble efforts.' Derbyshire folk have never been known for wrapping up their thoughts and opinions in over-diplomatic phrases!

Perhaps the best-known well-dressing village is Tissington. For centuries, Tissington's was the first of the Derbyshire well-dressings each year, though in 1970 Etwell village revived their dressings and chose mid-May, making them the new first in the well-dressing calendar. At Tissington five wells – the Hands Well, the Hall Well, the Town Well, the Yew Tree Well and the Coffin Well – were

Well dressing at Tissington: a Christianised form of pagan practice. (David Moorley)

dressed, though in 1982, a sixth, the Children's Well, was added. The opening ceremony always begins on Ascension Day with a service in the village church, and the pictures are left up for six days. Thousands of people from all over the world come to Tissington during these six days, and the quiet village becomes thronged with traffic and excited camera-wielding visitors.

So, given the church service and the Ascension Day connection, well-dressing is a Christian festival, surely. Well, historically speaking, no. Originally well-flowering was part of pagan worship. The wells and springs were sacred to goddesses and water sprites, and it was advisable to keep them happy by offering floral tributes. It was their due for keeping the water flowing, pure and plentiful during the year. In times of drought, it was the goddess of your village spring that kept life going. It was only sensible therefore to pay her respect, to make her offerings. It is possible that animal or even human sacrifices were made at one time, but flowers and offerings of growing crops proved a more acceptable tribute.

Some early Christians tried to ban these ancient practices. A decree of AD 960 banned the worship of fountains. In 1102, St Anselm condemned well-dressing as idolatry. But later the practice was absorbed into Christianity, with a few adaptations. The well at Buxton originally regarded as the spiritual home of the Celtic goddess Anu became St Anne's Well. That of the goddess Brigantea was renamed St Brigid's Well. A spring once dedicated to the water sprite Elen was now dedicated to St Helen.

However, in the minds of Derbyshire people, the wells still kept their supernatural properties. The waters of the newly Christianised wells were believed to cure all manner of diseases and afflictions. Those who drank the water would leave torn off pieces of clothing and ribbons attached to the wells, and it was not unusual for there to be crutches left there too, presumably no longer required by their now fully cured owners. This practice was frowned on during the Commonwealth period of Oliver Cromwell, and he had all the rags and crutches removed, and the wells locked away, though whether it was the Roman Catholicism of the practice or its pagan origins that annoyed him is open to conjecture.

The tradition of well-dressing is not a continuous historical line running from pagan times to the present day. According to one school of thought, the Tissington dressings date from 1615 when the wells there flowed through a prolonged drought, though another theory claims that they date back to 1349 when the purity of the water enabled villagers to survive the Black Death which swept through the county.

Another pagan tradition that lives on in Derbyshire is connected with elf-like creatures called hobs. These hobs could be tricky to deal with because they were extremely mischievous. If a farmer or his wife upset a hob, it would cause cows' milk to dry up or household crockery to break. However, if you kept on his good side, then crops would flourish and cows would give good yields of milk. In Derbyshire, the hob was frequently called Hob Hurst, the word *hurst* being a local term for a wood. The stories about this wood elf crop up all over the county, and at times merge into legends about the ubiquitous Green Man and even Robin Hood.

One such tale tells how a farmer from Chelmorton, near Buxton, was walking home one night when he saw a hob. He crept up behind it, seized it and put it in a sack. He wanted to take it home with him because it was widely believed that if you could tame a hob, it would perform all your domestic chores during the night. In return for doing your housework, all you had to provide was a daily bowl of porridge and a tankard of beer. As the farmer was carrying the sack home, the hob began to wail and shriek so piteously that the farmer felt sorry for it. He put down the sack and opened it. The freed hob fled to its lair, a cave below Topley Pike. That cave had a secret door within it, invisible to human eyes. The door was the entry to another world where hobs, fairies and goblins lived, but where human beings could never visit and return.

There are stories of cunning and foolhardy mortals finding their way into this secret world, but once there they were never allowed to leave. The cave became known as

Hurst House, though over the centuries it became corrupted into Thirst House.

Another Hurst House is to be found on Brampton Moor, a thousand feet above sea level. At Harland Edge, overlooking Chatsworth Park, is a round barrow burial mound, dating from the Bronze Age. This, too, was known as Hurst House and was believed to be the home of a solitary hob. In 1853, the barrow was excavated by Thomas Bateman and human bones were discovered. This immediately led to a macabre legend that this particular hob had an appetite for human flesh, and the bones were the remains of his meals!

One story where Christianity came head to head with the older religion occurred in the 1650s when a new parson was appointed to the church in the village of Derwent Woodland. This village disappeared in 1945 when the Ladybower Reservoir was created, though the ruins of its houses are occasionally seen during severe droughts when the water levels fall. In the mid-17th century a young unmarried clergyman came to the village to become the minister. His name was Jonathan Carter and he was one of the new breed of strict-living clergy appointed during the Commonwealth of Oliver Cromwell. He came from the village of Long Eaton, in the south-east of the county. Suffering from a weak chest, he had been advised that the cold air in the northern High Peak area would be better for his health, though that advice sounds somewhat kill-or-cure to me.

The Rev Jonathan Carter found the hard working farmworkers in his new parish to be good people, not wasteful or loose-living, people he could get on with. But he did criticise some of their beliefs and practices, which he said were not Christian but of heathen origin. Things came to a head when a group of villagers came to him to explain about a service they expected him to conduct, called the Sermon For The Dead.

'There is no such service,' the angry clergyman retorted.

'Oh yes, vicar,' they replied. 'On the first Sunday after Christmas, you go into the church just before midnight. At first you'll think there's nobody there, but as you look around you'll see some faces in the pews. There might be two or three of them. They will be transparent at first, but as they thicken up, you'll recognise them.'

'Ghosts, I suppose,' Jonathan snorted.

'Oh no, vicar,' his parishioners explained patiently. 'These are not dead people. They are the spirits of those villagers who will die in the next twelve months!'

The young parson exploded in fury. 'This is not Christian,' he shouted. 'You are all pagans in this village. I want no more to do with you and your heathen ways.'

What followed was one of those situations when a vicar and his parishioners are at loggerheads. He thought they were ungodly. They thought he was 'not one of us', a man from the south of the county who 'has come north to tell us what we can and can't do.' After all, his predecessor was a local man who had no problem with the local traditions. The villagers stopped going to church; some went to a neighbouring church, others just stopped going at all.

After the normal Christmas services, performed to one old lady and her dog, Jonathan began to worry what people might get up to on the Sunday after Christmas. He decided that he would be in church at midnight, not to hold any service, but to make sure that his heathen villagers were not conducting practices he would disapprove of.

In the gloom of the empty church, he climbed up into the pulpit from where he could keep his eye on the whole church. When the old church clock struck twelve, Jonathan looked around. As the final stroke died away, he saw something that sent a shiver down his spine. There *was* a face in the pews. He saw a second and a third. As the faces began to solidify, what he saw next made the very hairs on his neck stand up. Not only did he recognise the faces, he realised that one of them was his own. He stumbled through a quick blessing, then ran from the building. Back in the vicarage, he pulled the blankets over his head and tried in vain to sleep.

Over the days that followed, he spoke to his estranged parishioners, telling them that he had not meant to insult them with his criticisms. 'I will never agree with some of your ideas,' he said, 'but I have to admit that there are more things on earth than I fully comprehend. If I apologise for upsetting you earlier, is there some way we could all be friends again?' A truce was declared and people began to go to church again. The villagers returned to a happy way of life, but they were not surprised the following October when the vicar's bad chest came back. When he passed away, they simply said, 'We knew this would happen, because he told us that his was one of the faces he saw at the last Sermon For The Dead.'

Yet another example of Derbyshire's pagan legacy! But why have these traditions stayed on in Derbyshire rather than in other counties? In his book *Well-Dressing in Derbyshire*, Roy Christian suggests one possible reason. He writes, 'Some anthropologists believe that Celtic strains survived successive invasions of Romans, Saxons, Danes and Normans in the remote hills of the Peak, and that even today the true Peaklander is of Celtic descent. His culture may also have lingered on longer here than elsewhere.'

ENGLAND'S LAST REVOLUTION

———————— ✿ ————————

The Pentrich Rising, otherwise known as England's Last Revolution, took place in Derbyshire in 1817. The first two decades of the 19th century were a turbulent time. Conditions were hard, and working people and their families were suffering great hardship. The war with France had ended and soldiers were returning, adding to the unemployment and poverty that were already there. In 1815 the Corn Law was brought back to keep bread prices from falling, and in 1816 there had been a disastrous harvest. Derbyshire had falls of snow in early June and no grass grew until the end of that month. People could no longer afford to buy bread or potatoes. Hunger was everywhere and anger was widespread.

The government was in a state of panic. There had been two revolutions – one in France and a second in America – and conditions in England were ripe for a third. When the East Midlands became the centre of machine-breaking – the workers blamed the introduction of stocking and lace-making machines for their poverty – the government responded by making the breaking of machinery a specific hanging offence, along with the burning of hayricks, another so-called revolutionary activity.

Derby-born writer Edward Garner states: 'The ending of the war years saw a growing polarisation of society. Class differences were becoming more defined, adding to the government's growing unease.' Clarence Daniel of Eyam, in his book *A Peakland Portfolio*, says that 'the Derbyshire Rising was a short chapter in the long story of the class struggle in which the working man has repeatedly pressed his claim for fairer wages and better living conditions. It was a revolt against hunger, poverty and unemployment. It was a pathetic and ill-timed protest against the tyranny, inhumanity and misrule of a government entirely out of sympathy with the labouring classes.'

Some of the pressure for reform was channelled through political debating societies. Organisations known as Hampden Clubs sprang up all over the country, set up to discuss and to petition Parliament for social and political reform. Tom Paine's influential book *The Rights of Man*, published in 1795, was widely quoted. In Parliament, radical MPs like Lord Byron and Derbyshire's Sir Francis Burdett argued the case for social change, but the government continued to see all change as dangerous and all reformers as revolutionaries.

And there were those who believed that only direct action and armed rebellion would achieve the long-awaited improvement. One such was thirty-one year old Jeremiah Brandreth, an unemployed local framework knitter and former soldier with a charismatic personality and striking appearance. Jeremiah, born in Sutton-in-Ashfield and some-times nicknamed 'the Nottingham Captain', was described by a contemporary source as 'a high swarthy man with very black whiskers'. He was the leader of the men of Pentrich, near Ripley, who met to plan an armed rising against the hated government. The Derbyshire rebellion was to be, they firmly believed, just one part of a national revolution that would result in a march on London and the creation of a new government with Sir Francis Burdett of Foremark Hall in south Derbyshire as its prime minister. They had even designed a new flag, a red, white and green tricolour.

On Sunday 8th June 1817, a final meeting took place in the White Horse Inn in Pentrich, where the landlady was a widow, Ann Weightman, the mother of one of the rebels. Jeremiah Brandreth pointed to the map on the table and indicated the route the men would need to take to march first to Nottingham and then to London. He described where they would meet up with other parties of men with the same aim. They were to join contingents from South Wingfield, Alfreton and Crich the next night at Hunt's Barn, then march to Butterley where they would be reinforced by men from Sheffield and Chesterfield and seize the local ironworks. Some of the men had grievances with a local magistrate, Colonel Halton, and others with Mr Jessop, the owner of the Butterley ironworks. It was agreed that these two men would have to be shot. They would then be joined by parties from Codnor and Heanor in a march to Nottingham Forest and with the help of rebels from Nottingham they would seize that city.

Two of the men present were William Turner and Charles Swaine, who, like Jeremiah, were former soldiers. One of the government's fears was that soldiers returning from the Napoleonic wars would make common cause with the working-class poor, and bring their military expertise with them. Turner was the quartermaster, and he told the meeting that hidden in a quarry in Wingfield were forty pikes. Guns would be coming from both Wingfield and Ripley. They also had one barrel of gunpowder and a quantity of lead for making bullets. When asked what would happen when they ran out of lead, he said that there was plenty of lead on church roofs along their route.

Jeremiah got everyone present to chant his song:

> Everyone his skill must try
> He must turn out and not deny;
> No bloody soldier must he dread,
> He must turn out and fight for bread.
> The time is come, you plainly see,
> The government opposed must be.

One of the most enthusiastic of the revolutionaries at the meeting was a man known only as Oliver. He was the one who laughed at any of the men who expressed doubts. He was the one who encouraged Brandreth and Turner to go further with their ideas, turning romantic rhetoric into a real plan of action. Oliver was of genteel appearance, with a good speaking voice, standing erect at six feet tall, with light coloured hair and red whiskers. He wore a fashionable brown coat over a black waistcoat, dark blue pantaloons and black wellington style boots. He seemed a worthy recruit to the cause.

One of the leaders of the Pentrich group was absent from the meeting at the White Horse. He was Ann Weightman's brother, sixty-four year old Thomas Bacon, a keen reader of Thomas Paine, a self-educated and well-travelled man who had even visited America. Bacon had been a frameworker, and it is therefore highly likely that he had been connected with the Luddite movement. He had also worked at the local Butterley ironworks. He had been involved in the setting up of a number of Hampden Clubs, including the one at Ripley. The reason for Bacon's absence from the Sunday meeting at the White Horse is unknown.

The next day, Monday 9th June, a number of men made their way to Hunt's Barn in South Wingfield, among them Jeremiah Brandreth and George Weightman. Among the volunteers from the South Wingfield area were farmers Samuel and Daniel Hunt. Another was James Shipman, who inquired about the provision of food for the march, Jeremiah confidently assuring him that every man would receive bread, beef and rum. Asked about what would happen to their families, the ebullient leader said that once a provisional government had been formed their wives and children would receive all the food they needed.

At the barn, pikes, guns and ammunition were distributed, before the company split into two groups. One group went off to Wingfield Park where at the house of a widow, Mrs Mary Hepworth, Jeremiah Brandreth discharged his gun through a window and killed a servant, Robert Walters. This killing, which may well have been accidental, did cause some of the party to wonder what they were becoming involved in. The number of men was probably less than sixty at this time, and the total was constantly changing as more volunteers joined. It was not all one way: one farmer named Tomlinson deserted after the Hunt's Barn meeting and another rebel, Elijah Hall, left after the incident at the house of Mary Hepworth.

The two parties now rejoined and the two ex-soldiers, Will Turner and Charlie Swaine, marshalled the company, placing the men with guns at the front of a double file, and those with pikes at the rear. The little army, still numbering less than a hundred, marched to Butterley ironworks to try to recruit the six hundred and fifty men who were employed there. However, the manager, Mr Goodwin, refused to let Brandreth address his employees and warned the rebels that their enterprise would end upon the gallows. Surprisingly, Brandreth marched his men away without a shot being fired. It seems likely that he was keen to proceed with the march south, and could not spare the time to take the ironworks by force.

As the men marched off, a young recruit rode up with a bag full of lead bullets, badly needed by the band of revolutionaries. Goodwin dragged the man off his horse and took the ammunition from him. Even at this early stage, things were not going well for the rebels. Not only had the expected recruits from Chesterfield and Sheffield failed to appear, the weather had now turned to heavy rain.

The rather damp volunteers marched on to Ripley, where they were delighted by the sight of considerable reinforcements from Belper and Heage. In better spirits, the little Derbyshire army moved on to Codnor, where they took shelter in three public houses – the Glass House, the French Horn and the New Inn – while Will Turner and Sam Hunt went into the town to seek further recruits. Their mission proved successful and they returned with forty or fifty local men, then a further party of seventy arrived from Swanwick. Things were looking up. The army now numbered between two and three hundred.

At Langley Mill, they met up with George Weightman, who had been sent ahead to ascertain what was happening in Nottingham. His information was not encouraging; there had been very few rebels in Nottingham and these had easily been subdued by the military. After consultation with Jeremiah Brandreth, Weightman addressed the men, giving them a more encouraging report than the facts justified. If the falsified report was intended to raise the men's spirits, it was not wholly successful and there were several more desertions before the rebel army reached the racecourse at Nottingham Forest. After an encounter with the armed caretaker, the Derbyshire men continued towards Nottingham.

At Eastwood, a magistrate saw the advancing army and informed the military authorities. A party of the 15th Hussars marched out from Nottingham and, at 6 am, they met the rebels at Gilbrook. Brandreth formed his men up into a defensive line, but as the Hussars prepared to charge, many of the rebels broke ranks and fled. The remaining men, including Brandreth, stood firm but were soon routed. Forty men were taken there and then, and many more were arrested within a few days.

One of the first leaders taken was Will Turner, a forty-six year old stonemason from South Wingfield, who had seen sixteen years' service as a soldier. Isaac Ludlam, hunted down near Uttoxeter, was a fifty-two year old quarry owner and a noted Methodist preacher. George Weightman, the young sawyer whose mother kept the White Horse at Pentrich, was arrested near Sheffield. Jeremiah Brandreth managed to get to Bristol where he tried unsuccessfully to board a ship to America; eventually he returned to his wife and family in Nottinghamshire where he was soon taken into custody.

Thirty-five of the rebels were charged with high treason. At their trial in Derby, the prosecution was led by the Attorney General, Sir Samuel Shepherd, and the presiding judge was Sir Richard Richards. The jury of twelve local landowners knew what was expected of them and brought in the verdict required. Three men – Brandreth, Ludlam and Turner – were sentenced to death by hanging and post-humous beheading. Eleven others, including Thomas Bacon and George Weightman, were sentenced to transportation for life, and three more for fourteen years. A further six men were gaoled for periods between six months and two years. No evidence was produced in the case of the remaining twelve men, and these were freed.

Jeremiah Brandreth, Isaac Ludlam and William Turner were executed in Derby on Friday 7th November, outside the county gaol. On that day the three condemned men had their final communion in the prison chapel, and Jeremiah wrote a letter to his pregnant wife, Ann. They were taken to the scaffold on a hurdle, and then were publicly hanged before a crowd of Derby people.

Brandreth ascended the platform first, and addressed the crowd with the words 'God be with you all, all but Lord Castlereagh!' There are those who claim his words were 'God be with you all, and Lord Castlereagh', but this seems unlikely, given that Castlereagh was the most hated of the government ministers, and the most opposed to any kind of reform. (Indeed, the poet Shelley wrote of him 'I met murder on the way, He had a mask like Castlereagh.') Ludlam's final words were uncontroversial, but Will Turner proclaimed bitterly, 'This is the work of the government and Oliver.'

The three men were hanged from three nooses at 12.30 pm, watched by a crowd that included those prisoners awaiting transportation, who were marched out in chains to see their comrades die. Half an hour later, the bodies of the three men were hauled into a kneeling position and the platform covered with sawdust. One by one the necks of the three dead men were placed on the block. Jeremiah's head was the first to be severed, though the axeman failed to detach it cleanly and the gruesome task had to be completed by an assistant using a knife. The executioner held the bloody head aloft by its hair and proclaimed, 'Behold the head of a traitor, Jeremiah Brandreth.' By now the crowd were groaning and booing, and the soldiers present feared a civil disturbance. However, despite having to watch the same indignities committed on the bodies of Ludlam and Turner, the ceremony passed off without further trouble.

But why had William Turner referred to the government and *Oliver*? He was talking about the man who had seemed to be such a keen supporter of the Pentrich uprising. It soon became apparent that Oliver was not all he seemed. He had been present among the Derbyshire revolutionaries because he was being paid by the government to be there. His real name was probably William Oliver, though he was also known under the name W.J. Richards. He had been in prison

A contemporary print of the execution of Jeremiah Brandreth. (Derby Local Studies Library)

for debt and for bigamy, but these crimes had been wiped out when he became a government agent. With the information he was sending back to his paymasters, the Derbyshire revolt could easily have been nipped in the bud at an early stage, but for its own reasons the government decided to let it go on. They needed it to happen in order to put it down very publicly and very savagely.

Before the trial took place, the editor of the *Leeds Mercury*, Edward Baines, published an article, naming Oliver as a spy in government pay. Baines claimed that not only was Oliver a spy, he was also a driving force behind the rising, suggesting to the Derbyshire men that they take up arms. He was, in fact, a classic *agent provocateur*. A furious Sir Francis Burdett, the reform-minded MP from south Derbyshire, demanded to know why Oliver the spy had spread the tale that Burdett was to be the Prime Minister after the successful revolution. Had the government instructed their agent to misuse his name? Lord Liverpool conceded that Oliver was indeed their man, but denied telling him to name Sir Francis. Claiming that all governments had used spies and would always do so, Lord Liverpool said that on occasions such men would 'from zeal in their business' go too far.

During the trial, the legend 'REMEMBER OLIVER THE SPY' appeared on walls throughout Derby, in an attempt to remind the judge and jury of Oliver's part in the insurrection, but – unfortunately for the men on trial – Oliver never appeared in court. After the trial and execution, Oliver, now an embarrassment to his employers, was sent to South Africa, where he lived under the name William Oliver Jones. There he was given a sinecure, becoming the Inspector of Buildings in Cape Colony. He reverted to his previous criminal habits, however, regularly embezzling the money with which he was entrusted.

One further mystery remains, and that concerns Thomas Bacon. Despite not being physically present during the rebellion, Bacon was known to be a leader of the Pentrich men. However, he was not sentenced to death. Some historians have inferred from this that he too may have been in government pay. To me this seems extremely unlikely. Thomas Bacon had spent his whole life agitating for social reform, supporting the French and American revolutions, spreading the ideas of Thomas Paine. I do not see a man of his beliefs and principles selling out to the corrupt government of his time. And although he escaped the death penalty Thomas Bacon and his brother were transported for life. What is possible is that to convict him of being a leader of the insurrectionists, Oliver the spy would have had to give evidence in court. Now that was something the government was very keen to avoid.

It is sometimes claimed that the poet Percy Bysshe Shelley was present in Derby at the execution of Brandreth, Ludlam and Turner. There seems little factual evidence for this, though Shelley did write a political pamphlet entitled *We Pity The Plumage But Forget The Dying Bird*. In it, the poet contrasts the public mourning that followed the death of Princess Charlotte, daughter of the Prince Regent, with the apathy that followed the deaths of the leaders of the Derbyshire rising, whom he saw as victims of political intrigue. 'Fetters heavier than iron weigh upon us, because they bind our souls,' he wrote. 'Let us follow the corpse of British liberty slowly and reverentially to its tomb, and if some glorious phantom should appear . . . let us say that the spirit of Liberty has risen from its grave.'

As for Jeremiah Brandreth, he seems to have been a compelling personality but a naïve romantic. He firmly believed, or was persuaded by Oliver the spy, that the Pentrich Rising was one part of a mass rebellion that was occurring all over the nation. Indeed, he must have thought that the revolution was international since he told his followers at the Hunt's Barn meeting that the next day at 10 am a rising would take place in England, France and Ireland. He was wrong, however. Apart from a minor disturbance in Huddersfield, easily put down, it was only in Derbyshire that men actually took arms and rose against the corruption of their government. The Pentrich Rising was indeed England's last revolution, but it was, from the beginning, always doomed to fail. Thanks to Oliver the spy,

Lord Sidmouth, the Home Secretary, had known of the intended rebellion for many weeks before it happened. He even knew the date it was to occur; he could have stopped it, but chose to let it happen and be suppressed.

After the rising, the authorities continued to take action against those who might have supported the rebels. The village of Pentrich stood on land belonging to the Duke of Devonshire, and after the trial the Duke had many of its houses pulled down and their inhabitants turned out. Twenty of the 122 houses were demolished and the population of Pentrich was reduced from 726 to 508. It was no doubt hoped that pulling down the houses would mean that the memory of the rebels would also be wiped out.

The bodies of the three executed men were buried in an unmarked common grave in the churchyard of St Werburgh's in Derby. Although no monument to them exists, they are still remembered as part of Derbyshire working class history in both song and story. *The Liberty Tree*, a play based on the event, was performed in Derby in 1980. Singer-songwriters John Young and Keith Jones have written a number of songs about the Derbyshire men who took part in the Pentrich Rising, one of which concludes:

The fire that Brandreth kindled, today still burns as bright, That working men should organise and fight to get their rights.

Perhaps the attempt to annihilate the memory of those who took part in England's Last Revolution was less successful than the authorities hoped!

THE SIMMONDLEY
PIT MURDERS

———————— ✿ ————————

Albert Edward Burrows, who lived in the north Derbyshire cotton town of Glossop, was a big man with a quick temper. He had tried a variety of casual jobs: melting bitumen, farm labouring, and painting railway arches. His personality seemed a curious mixture of cruel and sentimental. On one occasion he brought home two young wild rabbits and built a hutch for them. The next morning, he got up early and took them back to the warren where he had found them because 'their mother will be fretting about them'. In contrast, when his landlady's dog went missing, Burrows brought its body home saying that he had found it dead in a rabbit hole. However, when the dog's lead was found in a water butt, together with some dog hairs, it was realised that he had drowned it.

By 1914, when Burrows was living with his wife and daughter, his outdoor interests included petty theft, poaching and spying on courting couples. Three years later, while working away from home in Cheshire, he met and fell in love with a twenty-seven year old woman called Hannah Calladine. Hannah had a young daughter, Elsie, from a previous relationship, but Burrows found her attractive and asked her to marry him, telling her that he was a widower with a daughter living in Glossop. The couple married in May 1918, and in October they had a baby son, also named Albert Edward. For a while, Albert senior ran two families, one in Cheshire and one in Glossop, and sent money to both wives. However, after the war ended, when many soldiers returned to civilian life, work became hard to find and the payments stopped.

Albert Burrows and Hannah Calladine: Burrows murdered
Hannah and her children in 1920. (Glossop Heritage Centre)

Hannah became suspicious, and wrote a letter to Burrows' daughter, asking whether the lady who looked after her really was just a housekeeper. Not surprisingly the girl passed the letter to her mother, and in February 1919 Albert Burrows was charged with committing bigamy. He was given a sentence of six months in prison, the judge saying that the lightness of the sentence reflected the fact that he had made financial contribution to both households when he was working.

When he came out of Liverpool prison in May, Burrows returned to Glossop to live with his legitimate wife and daughter, abandoning Hannah to try to bring up Albert and Elsie on her own. She obtained an affiliation order under which Burrows was to give her seven shillings a week, but he never made any attempt to pay it. As a result, he was arrested and sentenced to prison again, this time for 21 days in Shrewsbury prison.

In November, Burrows went to visit Hannah Calladine, who was by now living with her sister. Although he was refused entry to the house, he must have managed to meet her and, amazingly, to persuade her to try to make a go of it again. In December, Hannah left her sister's house and said that she was going to Glossop with her children. When she got there she went to the Burrows' house. Mrs Burrows was outraged, but took pity when she saw the exhausted and shivering children. Hannah, Elsie and little Albert were allowed to come in, and were told by Mrs Burrows that they could stay for one night only.

The next day, Burrows made what he no doubt thought was a wonderful suggestion. Why don't they all settle down together? Hannah could get a job to earn money while Mrs Burrows looked after all the children. Burrows would have both wives and both families in one house. Who could object to such a sensible solution? Well, Mrs Burrows did! When it became clear that Hannah and her children were there to stay, Mrs B took herself off to stay with a friend in Hollingcross Street.

In her absence, Albert Burrows settled down with

Police and workmen descend into the airshaft at Simmondley Pit. (Glossop Heritage Centre)

Hannah, Elsie and baby Albert. Although he couldn't find work, Hannah found a job in a paper mill. No doubt this arrangement seemed quite satisfactory to him, but this time it was his legitimate wife who took out a summons for maintenance. On 30th December, Inspector Chadwick called on Burrows and told him that he was to appear at a hearing on 12th January.

At the hearing, Burrows told the magistrates that the problem seemed to have solved itself, since Hannah had got a job in Manchester, and had left him, taking her children with her. Some of the neighbours thought that the disappearance of Hannah and her children was just too convenient. Burrows had been seen at six o'clock one morning walking along, holding the hand of little Elsie. Two hours later he was alone. When a neighbour commented about the early hour at which he had been seen, Albert replied that he was 'taking Elsie to be with her mother'.

Albert Burrows must have had some appeal, because four days later his wife moved back into his house with him. She may have thought it odd that Hannah had left some of her belongings behind, including her wedding ring. Burrows sold them all, and destroyed the papers and letters relating to her. This again led to some local gossip.

Eventually, the neighbours stopped discussing the whereabouts of Hannah and her children, and the Burrows family settled down into normality. Albert once again obtained casual farmwork, and took up his former habits of poaching and wandering the local countryside. He was a bit of a loner, with few friends, but one of his companions was a man called Tom Shortland, who suffered from poor sight and a speech impediment.

This relative peace and quiet was shattered in 1923 when a local boy, four year old Tommy Woods, disappeared. The youngster had left his home at 11 am on Sunday 4th March and had not been seen since. He was not missed until teatime, as his parents had assumed that he had gone to his grandmother's house for Sunday lunch. When they checked, his grandmother said that she had not seen him that day.

As the news spread, the community rallied round and all

the neighbours came to take part in the search. One of these neighbours was Albert Burrows, who lived in the same yard as the boy. He told a police sergeant that he had seen Tommy Woods at 12.30 pm on the Sunday, playing with a toy whip. He had warned the boy not to play on the road, and had last seen him with some older boys, leaning on the wall of a hen pen in Slatelands Road. He heard Tommy complain that the boys had thrown his purse into the pen. Albert added that the next day he had recovered Tommy's purse from the hen pen and given it to the boy's grandmother.

The police undertook a thorough search of the Slatelands Road area, and dragged the nearby Turnlee Brook. The boy's whip was found in the brook, but, strangely, it had been fastened to a heavy stone, almost as if it was intended to be found there. By Thursday, three hundred men – volunteers and police officers with dogs – were taking part in the search, which had spread into the hills and valleys towards Hayfield. One of the keenest volunteers was Albert Burrows but the policeman in charge, Inspector Chadwick, was somewhat cynical about his newfound public spirit. The inspector knew of Burrows' chequered criminal history and it was decided that he should be interviewed again.

Albert Burrows added more detail to his statement. Earlier on the Sunday, he had tramped across the fields to Hargate Hill, seeking a farmer named Clarkson who was looking for a farm labourer. However, the farm had proved too distant, and he returned to Bridgefield. On the way back, he had met and spoken to an off-duty policeman, Fred Bradbury. PC Bradbury was later to say that Albert Burrows had been sweating heavily although the day was cold and damp. Burrows said that he had arrived at Slatelands Road, where he had met his friend Tom Shortland. He said that he remembered pointing out little Tommy Woods with the older boys.

Tom confirmed this conversation, but it struck Inspector Chadwick as significant that the man Burrows was relying on to confirm that the missing boy was there at 12.30 was almost blind! He could remember seeing some boys dimly, and he could recall Burrows saying that Tommy Woods was with them, but there was no way that he could have seen the children clearly enough to recognise them for himself. The inspector was also convinced that Tommy Woods' toy whip had been placed in the brook by someone who wanted the police to think he had fallen in.

He was now sure that the child was in fact dead. The police enquiries continued, and on 9th March Chadwick interviewed a farm labourer named Sam Robinson. Sam stated that at 11.30 am on the Sunday, he had noticed Burrows at Bridgefield, holding the hand of a little boy. As the man and boy had not been seen on any of the roads in the area, the inspector concluded that Burrows and his young companion must have headed across the high moors overlooking Hargate Hill and Simmondley village.

Then Inspector Chadwick went to interview another farmworker, Frank Burgess, who had seen Burrows an hour later, on Hargate Hill. Together with a police sergeant, Inspector Chadwick visited Frank at Cloud Farm where he worked. The three men walked across the fields towards Hargate Hill. On the way, the inspector spotted an old airshaft belonging to a disused drift mine. He took a closer look and noticed that the 6 ft 6 ins wall around it had some loose stones. He removed a few, leaned through, and he could hear the faint sound of running water over 100 ft below. Frank told him that his employer regularly used the shaft to dispose of rubbish.

On Monday 12th March, Inspector Chadwick interviewed Burrows again, this time at the police station. The police officer accused the now agitated man of only pretending to be helpful in finding the boy, but in reality trying to mislead the police into believing the boy was alive after 12.30 pm. He mentioned that Burrows had been seen with the boy at 11.30, and demanded to know what he had done with him. Burrows went very quiet, then muttered that he had 'lost him' on the moors. His new story was that at 11 am on the Sunday in question he had seen Tommy Woods in Hollincross Lane. He had taken him for a walk to Bridgefield where they had met and spoken to Sam Robinson. He then took the boy across the fields looking for thrushes' nests. When they got up on the moors, he'd left Tommy sitting on his own while he went to try to find a rabbit. He was only about forty yards away, but when he returned the boy had gone. He searched and shouted for a few minutes before walking back. All his previous statements were lies, made up because he was frightened that he had lost the boy.

At the inspector's suggestion, Albert Burrows took him to the location where he claimed he had left the boy. It was a secluded spot with gorse and whimberry bushes growing on the moors above the village of Simmondley. In a ravine there was a tarn that was ten feet deep in places. Mr Wilkie, the chief constable, and two other officers joined the search and another airshaft was discovered. This one was not properly fenced off, except for a few wooden posts with rusty and broken barbed wire strands between them. A stone thrown into the shaft indicated that there was water at the bottom, so the officers sent for grappling irons and a rope. Attempts to use these were thwarted when the rope broke, and it was decided to resume the investigation the next day.

Burrows insisted on Inspector Chadwick accompanying him back to where he claimed to have left the boy, though this time the spot was a hundred yards from the one he had indicated originally. The nervous suspect kept asking, 'You don't think I have done him in, do you?' and insisting that he would never have harmed the boy. The two men retraced the route that Burrows and little Tommy had walked. When they got back, the officer allowed Burrows to go home, but made arrangements for him to be watched.

That evening, the inspector was thinking about the airshaft to be searched the next day and he suddenly remembered the other airshaft, the one near Cloud Farm. He recalled the loose stones that made an aperture in the wall. Could this shaft be connected with the boy's disappearance? Although not as isolated as the one on the moor, it might be an idea to have it checked while the police had the equipment. They could start with the Cloud Farm shaft, before ascending to the shaft on the moor.

The next day, word spread round the community that

lorries and policemen were heading towards Simmondley. By 11 am, the work had begun. Planks were placed across the shaft wall to form a platform, and the grappling irons were lowered down the airshaft. The first attempt produced only a large basket of ashes and refuse, but on the second go it could be seen that the hook was attached to the trouser leg of a small boy. Tommy Woods' body had been found. At the same time, a policeman approached Inspector Chadwick and informed him that Burrows was up on the hillside watching the operation. He sent a number of officers to apprehend the man.

Burrows had set out for the airshaft on the moors, but on hearing from some passers-by that the police were searching the shaft near Cloud Farm he had become very agitated and had set off across the fields to where he could watch the search.

As the news that Tommy Woods' body had been found spread through the neighbourhood, the public had no doubt who was responsible and a second, larger, posse – this one composed of irate locals wielding sticks – also began a hunt for Albert Burrows. He was spotted by a man named John Ambrey in a field about a mile away. John called his friends over, and Burrows' hands were tied behind his back. Fortunately, the police arrived just as his captors were using a scarf to try to hang him from an oak tree. Burrows must have been relieved when he was arrested by Detective Sergeant Wilson and taken into custody. He was put onto a lorry and transported to the police station, with the scarf – the would-be noose – still around his neck. The local populace lined the streets, and both Burrows and his police escort were pelted with missiles as well as threats the whole way. One woman left her ironing as she came out into the street and threw her flat iron at the lorry; luckily it did not hit Burrows or any of the policemen.

Once at the police station, the prisoner was bundled inside while the angry mob waited outside. The chief constable came out and announced that Burrows would appear before the magistrates the following day. The crowd reluctantly dispersed, deciding to let the law take care of him the official way. Many went home boasting that if the police hadn't arrived, they would have lynched the child-killer themselves. By next day, half the population were claiming that they had been there when the man was nearly strung up.

At the police station, Inspector Chadwick suddenly asked, 'Burrows, what became of Hannah Calladine?' Burrows replied that Hannah had obtained a good job in Manchester, working in a food shop. She earned good money, he went on, 'and doesn't come to me for any.' He then added, 'She often brings the children to see me.' The officer expressed surprise that no one else had seen her in Glossop since she went away. Burrows explained this by saying that she met him out on the moors. He then came out with the remarkable story that Hannah had been with him on the moors on the Sunday, and that was how little Tommy had got lost!

The next day, Burrows was remanded into custody, and at the inquest held the same day it was revealed that the boy had died of drowning and had been raped before his death. Burrows said that he was sixty-two and incapable of any sexual act, though most people knew he was ten years younger. Burrows still insisted that he had left the boy alive on the moor. He said that he must have fallen down the moorland airshaft and then been washed along underground to lie under the shaft where he was found. It was later proved that no subterranean link between the two shafts existed.

Albert Edward Burrows was charged with murder and sent for trial at Derby Assizes. With the prisoner safely in custody, Inspector Chadwick resolved to find Hannah Calladine and her two children. There was no sign of her at the Manchester provision shop where she was supposed to work; they had never heard of her. No local nursery had looked after the children. The inspector now began to think the worst, especially when he discovered that Hannah and baby Albert had last been seen with Burrows walking down Hollincross Lane. Burrows had returned alone at midnight, and had taken Elsie out the next morning 'to be with her mother.' Could the three of them be at the bottom of the same airshaft where little Tommy Woods had met his untimely death? It seemed feasible that Burrows had killed his 'wife' and their son, removed stones from the wall around the airshaft, thrown their bodies in, and then replaced the stones. The next morning, he could have thrown Elsie over the wall to be with her mother. This was the macabre scenario that the police officer had now to attempt to prove.

The police returned to the shaft where the boy's body had been found, and a more thorough investigation began. They knew that the trial of Burrows would begin in July, so it was imperative to proceed quickly. Initially the water and refuse was raised from the shaft using a bucket on a rope, but when it began to rain, the water was rising more quickly than it was being removed. A platform was installed just above the water at the bottom of the shaft. A steam pump was now used to lower the water level. Men would then descend the shaft and shovel stones and other material into a cradle that was raised to the surface by a winch. It was a slow and difficult task in unpleasant surroundings, and accidents occurred, one sending large stones down onto policemen working on the lower platform. Eventually, however, the contents of the cradle were found to include a portion of a child's skull and part of a woman's torso, with clothing attached to it. More human remains were discovered, including the tibia and fibula bones of a young girl, and an adult female skull. Examination of the teeth, together with the clothing, proved that these were the remains of Hannah Calladine and her two children.

On 4th July, Burrows appeared at Derby Assizes charged with the murder of four people: Tommy Woods on 4th March 1923, Hannah Calladine and her fifteen month old son Albert on 11th January 1920, and Elsie on 12th January 1920. Two factors stand out from these crimes as particularly horrendous. The fact that Elsie was killed a day after her mother and half-brother means that Burrows had taken her up to the airshaft and killed her the morning after the first murder, telling a neighbour in a chilling phrase that he had taken her 'to be with her mother'. And, of course, when he killed baby Albert he was murdering his own son.

For some reason, the prosecution decided to proceed with only two counts, the murders of Hannah and little Albert. The presiding judge was Mr Justice Shearman. Both the prosecution and the defence team had interesting juniors. The defender, Mr Norman Winning, MP, was assisted by Miss Cobb, the first female barrister to appear in a murder case. The prosecutor, Sir Henry Maddocks, KC, MP, had a lawyer named Norman Birkett as his second, a young man who was later to reach much higher status in his legal career.

The jury deliberated for only twelve minutes before bringing in a unanimous verdict of guilty. Albert Edward Burrows was sentenced to death, and in view of this, it was decided not to charge him with the murder of three year old Elsie and four year old Tommy Woods. He was hanged at Bagthorpe prison at 8 am on Wednesday 8th August 1923, five months after the death of little Tommy Woods. It is significant to note that if Burrows had not killed the boy, and thrown his body into the same airshaft where he had thrown the bodies of his three previous victims, then it is likely that he would have got away with what he had done.

These crimes, known around Glossop as the Simmondley Pit Murders, achieved national notoriety as 'the Derbyshire Pit Murders'.

SCOTTISH SOLDIERS AND MANCUNIAN VOICES

———————— ❁ ————————

Given the distance between Derbyshire and even the most southerly part of Scotland, it may seem bizarre that many of the ghosts and legends of Derbyshire have a Scottish connection.

The Scottish ghosts that haunt the old woodland churchyard near Chapel-en-le-Frith date back to 1648. At the battle of Ribble Moor, near Preston, the ten thousand strong Parliamentary army defeated the twenty thousand Royalist soldiers under the command of the Duke of Hamilton. A month after the battle, fifteen hundred Scottish soldiers who had been taken prisoner in the battle were brought south to the Derbyshire town of Chapel-en-le-Frith. They were hundreds of miles from home and in low spirits, but they would have been in an even worse state if they had known what awaited them.

They were taken to the tiny keepers' church in the forest, and were herded in like sheep. Once the fifteen hundred men were in, the doors were slammed shut, and locked. This occurred on September 14th, and it was not until September 30th that the doors were re-opened. The prisoners had spent sixteen days in terrible conditions, crammed upright and unable to move. It is not surprising that forty-four men were found dead on their feet when the church doors were eventually unlocked. Many more were too weakened to make the journey to Chester that their captors had planned. Those Scotsmen unable to travel remained in north-west Derbyshire but every one of them died soon afterwards. All the soldiers were buried in the churchyard of the building that had been their prison and their hellhole.

Although the 13th century church in which the atrocity took place was pulled down and replaced in the 18th century, the churchyard containing the remains of the Scottish soldiers is still there. Everyone who visits experiences the melancholy atmosphere of the place, and some have reported hearing the sound of groaning men. Robert and Betty Prior of Derby say that when they went there in September 1998, they heard a Scottish lament being sung by the voice of a young boy. Betty is convinced that the singer must have been one of the soldiers who met his death in 'the black hole of Derbyshire' over 350 years earlier.

Scottish soldiers returned to Derbyshire almost a hundred years after that terrible event. In 1745, Charles Edward Stuart, known as Bonnie Prince Charlie, marched south from Scotland to reclaim the English throne for the Stuart cause. In the Derbyshire town of Ashbourne, he proclaimed his father as James III, the true king of England. Charles then proceeded to Derby, but an advance guard of soldiers pressed a few miles further to Swarkestone to take and hold the bridge over the River Trent.

While in Derby, Prince Charlie held a council of war, but his chief military advisor, Lord George Murray, strongly advocated that they should not try to advance any further towards London. Against his own better judgement, Charles followed his advice and the long slow retreat back to Scotland began. As they headed north, the Scottish soldiers were continually harried by the troops of George II, and many of them were killed or captured. There is a strong local belief that Hanging Bridge, just west of Ashbourne, got its name because of the Scottish soldiers who were hanged there. Although historians usually dismiss this legend, almost everyone in that part of west Derbyshire believes it to be true.

In 1960, Alan Henton was visiting his aunt in Swarkestone and went out to take her dog for a walk. He was crossing Swarkestone Bridge, which today consists of not only the bridge over the river but also a long narrow causeway over the floodplain, when he heard the sound of many horses and riders approaching. He pulled his dog into one of the recesses in the wall of the bridge, normally used by pedestrians trying to avoid the traffic. Although the sound of the horses came nearer, passed the spot where he stood, then continued over the bridge, Alan saw nothing. He says that his aunt's dog was cowering down in fear, so after the sounds had died away, Alan turned back towards his aunt's home. On the other end of the bridge he met a lady who said she had heard nothing of the sounds. However, when he got home and told his aunt what he had heard, she reassured him that it was a common occurrence. 'Oh, don't worry,' she said, 'it's only the ghosts of Bonnie Prince Charlie's soldiers. Lots of people have heard them.' If Alan had been in the same location today, he might have had a clue to the ghostly sounds, since the large newly-built pub about a mile from the bridge has been named the Bonnie Prince.

When the film star Diana Dors went to Ashbourne one summer day in 1962, she too had a strange experience. She was there to open a fete to raise funds for St Monica's Church of England children's home. After the fete, she was staying the night at a 16th century cottage just west of Ashbourne, but her sleep was disturbed when she awoke in the early hours of the morning. There in front of her was a long-haired and bearded figure, wearing a kilt!

Now Diana was a very pretty girl and no doubt was used to being pestered by love-struck males, but this apparition was entirely grey. It had grey clothing, grey hair and grey skin. As Diana stared in horror, the ghost slowly faded away. She admitted to a local newspaper that she had been frightened of the horrible figure at the time, but the next day decided to investigate further. She was told by the owner of the cottage that he had been seen before, and that he was the ghost of a Jacobite soldier captured and killed in the area as Bonnie Prince Charlie's men retreated through Derbyshire. Diana became convinced that she had seen just one of the many Scottish ghosts that haunt different areas of Derbyshire.

The ghosts heard by schoolteachers Joe and Rachel Cohen

in 1952, however, had not Scottish but Manchester accents and there were hundreds of them. They had set out from Hayfield to walk up Kinder Scout one Sunday in the Easter holidays when they heard the sound of many people singing. The couple, both members of the Labour Party, recognised the song immediately as *The Red Flag*. Thinking that a party of socialist ramblers were in the vicinity, they tried to find them, but failed. What puzzled Joe and Rachel was that it sounded as if there were dozens if not hundreds of singers, yet all they could see on the hillside were a few walkers in one and twos, and they were definitely not singing. Interestingly, the other walkers all seemed to be looking about them as if they too were wondering about the source of the music.

This strange phenomenon seems to have repeated itself thirty years later, when three teenage boys from Wales heard mysterious singing 'like a male voice choir' in approximately the same spot. Again the source of the singing proved elusive. At the Youth Hostel where they were staying the boys tried to reproduce the song they had heard by whistling and humming, and, after playing 'Name That Tune' for some time, fellow hostellers finally decided that what these three had heard was *The Internationale*.

The warden of the hostel informed the youths that fifty years earlier, Kinder Scout had been the site of a struggle between five hundred Manchester ramblers and thirty keepers employed by the then Duke of Devonshire to keep trespassers off the mountains. Although the latter were armed with clubs and sticks, the unarmed ramblers won the day and marched on to Ashop Head, where they met up with ramblers from Sheffield. They held a meeting, then marched back to Hayfield, where a large force of policemen were waiting for them. As a result of the mass trespass, a number of the ramblers appeared before a judge and jury at Derby Assizes. The jury, far from being composed of twelve of the accused ramblers' peers, was made up of two brigadier generals, three colonels, two majors, three captains, two aldermen and three other landowners. Unsurprisingly, five of the trespassers – John Anderson, Benny Rothman, Tony Gillet, Jud Clyne and

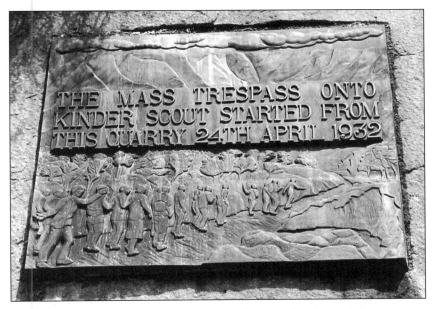

Plaque at Hayfield commemorating the Kinder Scout Mass Trespass of 1932. (David Moorley)

Dave Nussbaum – were sent to prison for periods of between two and six months. The latter received an extra month for selling copies of the *Daily Worker*.

Many of the ramblers were members of the British Workers' Sports Federation and other socialist organisations in Manchester, making a stand for people to have the right to walk the Derbyshire hills. It is highly likely that *The Red Flag* and *The Internationale* would have been among the songs sung that day in 1932. The event was celebrated in the song *The Manchester Rambler*, written by Ewan McColl and containing the immortal lines: 'I may be a wage-slave on Monday, but I am a free man on Sunday.'

The action taken in 1932 gave birth three years later to the Ramblers' Association. The event was also the direct forerunner of the establishment of national parks – the first of which was the Peak District, created in 1951 – and the Countryside and Rights of Way Act passed in 2001. In April 2002, at an anniversary meeting of ramblers held at

Hayfield, the present Duke of Devonshire apologised for the actions of his grandfather. He said that he was horrified both by the attitudes of the landowners of the time, including the ninth Duke of Devonshire, and by the severity of the sentences handed down to the arrested ramblers.

Also present at the anniversary ramble was Jimmy Jones, one of the few surviving participants of the original event, having then been a fifteen year old member of the Young Communist League. Jimmy commented, 'We all supported the trespass because we were convinced that the land belonged to the people. It was in our blood.' Jimmy recalled that at the original ramble he had been accompanied by his father and twenty year old Benny Rothman. Benny, one of the organisers of the trespass, died in January 2002, three months before the seventieth anniversary celebrations.

But how can the singing heard in 1952 and 1982 be explained? Was it the ghosts of the original marchers? This idea would have been rejected by many of those rational good comrades of 1932, but one possible explanation was given to me by a farmer from the Ilkeston area. He recalled an event in his own life when he heard noises on his farm that echoed an event that had taken place six months earlier. He is convinced that the land can absorb sounds and in some strange way replay them, though he does not know what triggers this. His suggestion is that the sounds of the momentous events of April 1932, the singing and the fighting, were absorbed into the rocks of Kinder Scout and have been recreated at intervals ever since!

A GRANDMOTHER'S BATTLE FOR JUSTICE

———————— ❀ ————————

During my career as a primary school teacher, on several occasions I came across children who had been reared by their granny. The usual scenario was that the child had been born to a young unmarried girl, and her parents had rejected the idea of adoption (or termination), choosing instead to bring up the baby within the family. In my experience, these granny-reared children were invariably well balanced and sensible, regarding granny as mum and biological mum as big sister, though usually in full knowledge of the real facts. I always found these children a credit to their family.

Lynn Siddons was lucky to have been brought up in this type of family. She was born when her mother Gail was sixteen. Lynn was a healthy baby, weighing nearly 8½ lbs, which must have made a difficult birth for Gail who was only 4 ft 10½ ins. Gail had kept her pregnancy secret for six months, then told her mother, Flo. It was Flo who had to break the news to her husband, Fred. He had some difficulty accepting the fact, but once the baby was born, he became a doting granddad-cum-father to her. But it was battling Flo Siddons – herself only 5 ft tall – who went round to confront the married man who had got her daughter into trouble, to give him a piece of her mind.

The Siddons were a close and happy family and Lynn was raised in the family home in Carlyle Street, in the Sinfin area of Derby. Although Lynn was told the true relationships from the beginning, she always called Flo mam, Fred dad, and her real mum Gail. When Gail got married some years later, Lynn opted to stay with Flo and Fred, her 'mam and dad', though she spent many weekends and her holidays with Gail and her new husband John.

Lynn was known on the estate where she lived as a kind and caring girl, always ready to go and sit with elderly neighbours, or do their shopping.

Although she was bright, Lynn didn't take school very seriously. She was good at Art and English, and was a star of the hockey and rounders teams. She left school in April 1978, when she was sixteen. She was due to start work in the local Co-op butchers, but was determined to enjoy the Easter holiday first.

On Easter Monday, she went clothes shopping in Derby with her Aunt Cynthia and Flo. At about midday, Lynn returned to Sinfin, leaving her gran and aunt still shopping. She was hoping that her boyfriend Bobby would be calling for her during the afternoon, before taking her to the fair that night.

When Bobby didn't turn up, Lynn decided to go round to see her friend Roy Brookes at number 27. Roy was, at fifteen, only a year younger than Lynn but he looked about

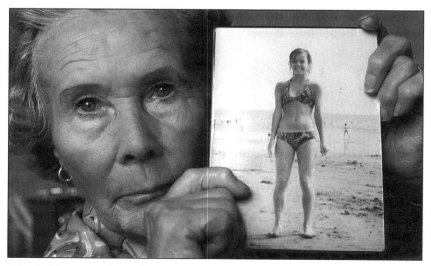

Flo Siddons with a photograph of her murdered granddaughter, Lynn. (Derby Telegraph)

twelve. Lynn got on well with Roy's mum Dot but found his stepfather Mick rather creepy. She would have been even more wary of Mick Brookes had she known of his disturbing practice of cutting out pictures of nude women, then stabbing them with knives and darts.

Lynn was a good friend to Roy, always sticking up for him when the other children on the estate teased him because of his size or started name-calling because of his mixed race (Roy's own father was from Dominica). When Lynn called round on the Monday afternoon, Roy asked her if she would walk with him through Red Wood and along the canal bank to find a farm where, according to his stepfather, they were looking for a boy to work part-time. Lynn agreed and the two youngsters set out. Mick Brookes watched them go, then set out the opposite way down the street. Lynn was never seen alive again.

When Flo and Cynthia returned from shopping, they realised that Lynn had not gone to the fair, as her purse was still in the house. Wherever Lynn had gone, Flo fully expected that she would soon be home, since she always left a note if she was going to be out for long. When she enquired at the Brookes house, Roy told Flo that after crossing the golf course with Lynn, he had nipped into Red Wood for a pee, but when he came out Lynn had gone off without him. Flo found this very odd, since the wood was surrounded by fields and Roy should have been able to see Lynn, even if she had decided to go off.

Flo began to ring round the members of her family and they all gradually rallied at her Carlyle Street home. At 10 pm they decided to go to the police, but found that the news of a sixteen year old girl going missing on the night of Easter Monday did not cause any immediate alarm. The uniformed policeman who called told them that thousands of teenagers went missing every week and they always turned up after a few days. Besides it was too dark to start looking that night, so any search would have to wait until morning.

At 2 am Flo's sons Keith and Barrie took the dog out for a search with torches. They walked the estate roads, then set out to Red Wood, but returned two hours later having found nothing. The next day, a policeman made a search in the same spot but he too found nothing. The police still refused to take Lynn's disappearance seriously, insisting that she had almost certainly run off with her boyfriend. When Flo insisted that Lynn wouldn't have caused her family distress in that way, the police officers smiled and explained that the families of missing teenagers always said the same thing.

Roy Brookes, when questioned, stuck to his story, but later added that he had seen a white car near the wood at the time when Lynn had gone off. This struck Flo as very bizarre, since there were no roads to the woods. Flo became annoyed when Mick Brookes began to sneer that Lynn wasn't the good little girl everyone thought. What really riled her was when he alleged that Lynn used to sneak out and spend the night with her boyfriend 'in an empty house in Harrington Street'. Flo knew that this was a lie, since Lynn had slept with her since Fred's death a few months earlier. She wondered why Mick was so keen to blacken Lynn's name.

With the police still unwilling to go public with the news of the girl's disappearance, the Siddons family took action themselves, making copies of Lynn's photograph and taking them round the stallholders and punters at the fairground. They were getting nowhere, however, and were desperately unhappy at the lack of progress. Then late on the Thursday evening, Bobby Muir, Lynn's boyfriend, turned up at Flo's house with a friend. Bobby said he had come to see what help he could be, and explained that he had been keeping a low profile because the police wanted to interview him over some petty thieving. Flo believed the boy, but decided to keep him talking while Gail rang the police. Bobby was taken in for questioning, but was released when it became obvious that he was unconnected with Lynn's disappearance.

Still exasperated by the lack of publicity their plight was getting, Cynthia approached her MP, Phillip Whitehead, at one of his surgeries. Phillip, a former television producer and journalist, was appalled at the delays and agreed to use his influence. The next day, a Saturday, the *Derby Evening Telegraph* made Lynn's disappearance its front page story.

Flo Siddons and her family drew the early conclusion that if the authorities are not doing enough, the answer is to do it for yourself.

Lynn's body was discovered the next day by an off-duty Metropolitan police cadet who was on leave staying with his mother in Derby. Seventeen year old Ian Hardwick was out cycling with his brother and another friend. They had parked their bikes and were walking along the towpath of the Trent and Mersey Canal, when Ian found Lynn's body hidden in thick undergrowth. As a police cadet, Ian knew what to do: touching nothing at the scene he cycled off to find someone to phone the police.

When the police arrived their initial thought was that Lynn had been killed with a shotgun, but it was then realised that she had suffered multiple stab wounds. A subsequent post mortem would reveal that the stab wounds fell into two categories; some were deep wounds penetrating four inches into Lynn's body, but others were mere pinpricks.

After the Siddons family had been informed that a body had been found and it had been identified as that of Lynn, officers went to 27 Carlyle Street and took Roy Brookes in for questioning. After repeating his earlier statement, Roy broke down, sobbing uncontrollably and unable or unwilling to answer their questions. The police were getting nowhere, and made the decision – wrongly as things were to turn out – to allow him ten minutes alone with his stepfather 'to calm him down'.

After the conversation with Michael Brookes, Roy said that he was now willing to talk. He said that he had killed Lynn Siddons when she had taunted him sexually and racially during their walk. He had acted alone, and nobody had witnessed the attack. The police decided that they had got the killer and Roy Brookes was charged. No one seemed to have any doubts as to how a young boy weighing less than six and a half stone and little over five feet in height could subdue a fit young woman four inches taller than himself. Even when the coroner's report revealed that Lynn had been strangled from behind as well as stabbed, the police still continued to press ahead with charging Roy

Brookes – and Roy Brookes alone – with the murder.

In the months that followed, Roy Brookes, on remand in the juvenile wing of a Midlands prison, became more and more withdrawn, refusing to talk to his solicitor. It was decided to bring in a psychiatric consultant from the Pastures Hospital at Mickleover in order to communicate with the boy. Dr Tom Dorman gradually built up Roy's confidence and an entirely new scenario began to emerge. Roy told Dr Dorman that he had invited Lynn to walk with him at the specific instruction of his stepfather, Michael Brookes, who had told him that his mother Dot would be harmed if he did not get Lynn to walk with him down to the canal.

Michael Brookes had caught up with the two teenagers and walked with them along the canal path. Suddenly, Michael had grabbed Lynn from behind, holding her by the mouth. He produced a carving knife and told Roy to stick it in her. Terrified, Roy made tentative attempts to do so, but pulling his punches so that Lynn wouldn't be too hurt. As his stepfather grew angrier, Roy managed to draw the knife sideways, causing its handle to break off. Michael Brookes now produced another knife, plunging it deep into the teenage girl's body.

This new information was offered to the police, but they dismissed it as an attempt by Roy Brookes to implicate someone else. When the trial took place in November, Roy Brookes was the accused and Michael Brookes was a witness for the prosecution. However, it soon became all too apparent that Roy could not have murdered Lynn Siddons on his own. He was too light, too small, to have killed the much stronger and much fitter girl. As the jury heard the forensic evidence of Lynn being held from behind, and of the two distinct types of stab wounds, it was clear that Roy's second statement – naming his stepfather as Lynn's killer – was the only one which fitted the facts.

After a four day trial, the jury took only twenty minutes to find Roy Brookes not guilty of murder, and the judge said that he agreed with their verdict. Mr Justice Mais ordered Roy to be taken to a place of safety for his own protection.

And Michael Brookes just went home!

To the amazement of the Derby public and the fury of the Siddons family, that was how the matter rested for year after year. Remembering the earlier lesson that if the authorities will not act, then you do it for yourself, Flo and her family organised petitions and marches. Posters were put up all over Derby. When these tactics failed the family began a vendetta against the Brookes family, driving them first from Sinfin, then from Macklin Street in the city centre. Some of the campaign was reasonable, Flo standing outside Michael Brookes' house silently for fifteen minutes every morning before she went to work, but at times it became more violent. Windows were broken, graffiti painted on doors. In 1980, Flo's daughter Cynthia was prosecuted for attempting to run down Michael Brookes in her car. Originally charged with attempted murder, she was actually found guilty of reckless driving and fined £100 with £300 costs. The Siddons family remained close and determined and had no compunction about the campaign of harassment against Michael Brookes. To them it was a black and white issue: Brookes had murdered Lynn, everyone knew he was guilty but nothing was being done about it.

Throughout the whole period, despite interventions from Phillip Whitehead, MP, the police continued to say that there was insufficient evidence to charge Michael Brookes. Not that they were very careful with evidence when it was discovered. The tenant who took over 27 Carlyle Street found a knife blade buried in the garden. He informed the police who sent a uniformed constable over to collect it, but incredibly the police managed to lose it. Partially burnt clothing, including a shirt, trousers and a shoe, were also dug up in Mick Brookes' former garden. These too were taken to the police station, but again were mislaid!

A breakthrough seemed to have been made in 1980 when Mick Brookes made the fatal mistake of leaving his wife Dot for a younger woman. Hell has no fury like a woman scorned. Dot contacted the Siddons, and three women – Flo, Gail and Cynthia – went to visit her. Dot told them that Brookes had confessed to murdering Lynn, and that she was willing to make a statement. The Siddons' solicitor arranged for a retired police officer, Ossie Lloyd, to visit Dot Brookes and the statement was taken down and signed. In it Dot told how Michael Brookes had confessed to the murder, before burning the clothes he had been wearing that day. He said that Roy had been present but had been trembling and useless. When Dot had asked him why he had done it, Michael Brookes had said that Lynn was 'a slut, like the rest of them'. Dot also told of her husband's peculiar habits, pinning up pictures of naked women and throwing knives at them. He liked her to lie half-dressed across their bed while he pretended to stab her.

Dot made a similar statement to Phillip Whitehead's researcher, and this was immediately handed over to the police. It seemed to Flo Siddons that the police were bound to act, but things went wrong. Once he heard about his wife's statement, Michael abandoned his new girlfriend and returned to Dot. In return, Dot withdrew her statement. The stalemate resumed. The atmosphere in Derby forced the Brookes family to flee the city, to live in Peterborough.

In 1981, the campaigning journalist Paul Foot became involved, using his column in the *Daily Mirror* to review the case. Although Paul is best known for defending people he believes to have been wrongly convicted, on this occasion he weighed in on the side of the Derby family who were being denied justice. Using the court case where Cynthia had been found guilty of reckless driving, Paul Foot was able to give the background to the case and – most importantly – to name Michael Brookes. The story was not challenged by the Brookes family or their solicitors; no writ for libel was issued as some of the *Mirror* executives had feared. Paul Foot stated that his intervention was justified because of 'the incompetence of the police, the battle for justice by this determined family, but most of all, you had a murder where everyone knew the suspects but they were still free.'

Paul Foot became very fond of Flo Siddons, the battling five foot Derby grandmother, and he gave her the name of a young idealistic and enthusiastic solicitor, Jane Deighton, who might be interested in helping with her campaign. Jane eventually came up with a breathtakingly innovative idea. The Siddons family could pursue a civil case for battery against Michael and Roy Brookes, claiming damages for causing Lynn's death. Charging them with battery rather than murder would avoid the complications that a civil case for murder would involve. The first problem to be solved was financial. The Siddons family had already paid many legal bills, Flo working as a cleaner to raise the money. To Flo's disgust, they had been awarded the princely sum of £27 from the Criminal Injuries Board for Lynn's death.

Good news came when an application for Legal Aid was granted, but more money was needed. Flo was not happy with the idea of a public appeal for cash – that would have been like begging – but the people of Derby rallied to the cause by organising fund-raising events: a sponsored walk from Derby to Matlock, raffles, jumble sales, sponsored events in pubs. It was now ten years since the murder, but Derby people have long memories and big hearts. The money was raised, and in 1989 the case was ready to go to court.

All the hopes were dashed, however, when Mr Justice Schiemann ruled that the case should have been brought within three years of the event, adding that the whole thing was 'financially pointless' since the defendants would have no assets to meet any judgements against them. Fortunately, a year later, an appeal against this ruling was allowed, and the case eventually came to court in July 1991. It was the first time ever that a civil claim for damages had been heard where no one had been convicted of the crime.

This time the judge, Mr Justice Rougier, was sympathetic. He pointed out that, although the case alleged battery, its effect was to accuse the defendants of murder. When the Derbyshire police refused to release statements and evidence on the grounds that it might prejudice any future prosecution, the judge overruled them and ordered the documents to be produced. Perhaps, like the people of Derby, he thought that 13 years was more than enough time for the evidence to remain hidden. When the solicitors for Michael Brookes objected to Roy Brookes giving evidence against his stepfather, the judge ruled against them.

Roy Brookes admitted that he had been 'persuaded' by his stepfather to lure Lynn onto the canal path on the afternoon of 3rd April 1978. He described how Michael had seized Lynn and had stabbed her to death after Roy had failed to do as instructed. He said that Michael had then filled Lynn's mouth with mud, and hidden her body in the undergrowth. He also said that Michael had told him that he wanted to kill more women than Jack the Ripper. Other witnesses gave evidence of Michael's obsession with stabbing pictures of women. The lawyers acting for Michael Brookes decided not to call him to give evidence.

On 30th September 1991, Mr Justice Rougier gave his judgement with the words, 'I won't keep you in suspense any longer. I find for the plaintiffs.' He said that at the time of the murder, Michael Brookes was in the grip of a demonic frenzy, adding that Roy played a part in the killing under duress. His judgement was that Michael Brookes was 80% liable and Roy Brookes 20% liable for the pain and terror inflicted, but that Michael was 100% liable for any damages, which were assessed at £10,641. To Flo Siddons and her family any damages were academic; this case was never about money. It was about justice.

But would a criminal case ever be brought? Some factors had changed. There was a new chief constable in Derbyshire, John Newing, who might have less reason for defending the actions that his force had taken long before his time. There was a new director of public prosecutions, Barbara Mills, QC, who might see the possibility of a case proving successful. And of course there was now a judgement in a civil case finding Michael Brookes guilty of Lynn's murder.

In 1992, Derbyshire detectives went to Michael Brookes' Peterborough home, and he was arrested for the murder. Four years later, *eighteen years* after the crime, Michael Brookes appeared at the Old Bailey, on a charge of murdering Lynn Siddons. After a thirty-four day trial, at which Roy Brookes was the chief witness and Michael Brookes refused to give evidence, the jury retired for almost

nine hours before bringing in a guilty verdict. Mr Justice
Mitchell passed the sentence, and Michael Brookes went
down for life.

Nothing could bring back the dead girl, but battling Flo
Siddons and her family had achieved what they had always
sought – justice. I'm not sure that I believe in such notions,
but if there is such a thing as an avenging angel I would not
be surprised if she was about five feet tall and pursued
vengeance with a Derby accent.

WITCHCRAFT IN DERBYSHIRE

———————————❖———————————

Witches have been ill-treated by the authorities – including the church – during much of this country's history. They have been harassed, arrested, tortured, and sentenced to death. Despite the myths and several historically inaccurate films, witches in England were executed by hanging, with burning at the stake being reserved for heretics (i.e. being a Roman Catholic under Henry VIII or a Protestant under Queen Mary). One such example was Joan Waste of Derby who was burned at the stake in 1556, suffering that terrible fate for the heresy of denying that the bread and wine taken at mass was literally turned into the flesh and blood of Christ. Joan had been blind from birth and had to be led to the stake by her brother Roger. She was a martyr or a heretic, depending on your point of view, but certainly not a witch.

It might be useful to decide who these dreaded witches were. They could occasionally be male, but the term 'witch' was predominantly applied to females. It is sometimes argued that they were a surviving remnant from the older pre-Christian religion, paganism, but I think the vast majority of them must have just been women who lived alone. If they had some knowledge of the medical properties of herbs and plants, this made them suspect in an atmosphere when the official church attitude to illness was that it was sent from God. Attempting to cure it was obviously flying against the will of the Almighty. It followed that the knowledge of the curative effect of herbs could not come from God so it must come from his arch-enemy – Satan. If these wise women also kept a pet – a cat or a tame raven, for example – and even spoke to the animal, this was additional evidence that they were witches. They were communicating with the Devil by means of his messengers, who came disguised as animals. If any old women suffered from hallucinations, or talked to themselves, or were simply old, ugly or behaved in any strange manner, they were in imminent danger of being regarded as witches.

Derbyshire had its fair share of witches. In February 1596, a boy called Thomas Darling managed to get lost in Winshill Woods, on the Derbyshire side of the county border with Staffordshire, close to Burton-upon-Trent. Tom was very frightened and he wandered aimlessly for hour after hour in a state of near panic. It was getting dark before he eventually came across a footpath, which he followed. Once out of the wood he returned home where his alarmed parents greeted his appearance with joy and relief.

Tom quite enjoyed all the attention from his family, and this increased when he appeared to suffer a series of fits. He began to talk in a rambling manner, saying that in the wood he had seen a green cat and a number of green angels. His fame spread through the neighbourhood, so he added a fantastic story of seeing a large man emerging from a chamber pot. To his surprise he was taken seriously, managing to get away with vulgarities that would normally have been reprimanded, so he added that in the chamber pot he had also seen the flames of hell and the heavens opening.

Doctors were called and diagnosed him as suffering from fits, but Tom heard his family saying that in their opinion he appeared bewitched. Once witches were mentioned, Tom suddenly said that he now remembered meeting a witch in the woods. She was a little old woman with warts on her face. In fact, now he thought about it, she was Mother Goodridge, naming an old woman who lived in Winshill. Tom came out with a story that as she walked past him in the woods he had farted and she had put a curse on him saying he would go to hell.

Tom's tale was believed and Alice Goodridge was taken into custody for questioning. She confirmed that she had met Tom Darling a few days previously and when he broke wind and laughed about it, she had reprimanded him about his rude behaviour. In response, Tom had called her an old witch. Alice said that her reply to him was, 'Every boy doth call me witch, but did I make thy arse to itch?'

Mother Goodridge was arrested and charged with witchcraft. She was tortured and humiliated. Her whole body was shaved so that she could be examined for any physical signs of witchcraft, such as a blemish known as the Devil's kiss. Her tortures included having iron shoes heated on a fire and forced onto her feet. In her agony, Alice eventually cried out that she would reveal everything if they would remove the shoes. Once they were off, however, she said she had nothing to confess. Subsequent torture led her to admit that the Devil had come to her in the form of a dog, and had led her into practising witchcraft. Although Thomas Darling later admitted that he had faked both the fits and the revelations, Alice was sentenced to a year in Derby gaol, where she died.

Even less fortunate than Alice Goodridge was a Bakewell milliner, Mrs Stafford, accused of witchcraft in 1608. A watchman found a Scottish tramp hiding in the cellar of a house in London. He was charged with vagrancy and intended robbery, and in his defence, he came out with a fantastic tale. He was not in the cellar of his own free will but had been transported there 'like the wind' through witchcraft. His story continued that he had been a lodger in the house of a milliner in Bakewell in Derbyshire. One night he had awoken to find a bright light shining through cracks in the floorboards from the room below. He got out of bed and peered through the largest crack. There in the room below was his landlady, Mrs Stafford, and her sister getting ready for a journey. He heard Mrs Stafford chant, ' Over thick and over thin, now Devil, to the cellar in London.' The two women then disappeared, only to reappear some time later carrying stolen material. He waited until they had gone to bed, then went down to the same room. The tramp then tried to cast the same spell himself, saying, 'Through thick and through thin, now Devil, to the cellar in London.' He too was transported all the way from Bakewell to London, but because he had said *Through thick and through thin* rather than *Over thick and over thin,* he had been carried by a mighty wind through every hedge and ditch, every bush and tree, on the journey. 'And that, your honour,' he concluded, 'is how I came to be in this cellar!' He added that if they checked at the milliner's house, they would find his clothes and other property still there where he had left them.

Instead of dismissing this story as a fantasy and a specious excuse, the authorities sent word to Bakewell, and Mrs Stafford's house was entered and searched. Sure enough, the tramp's belongings were found there. Despite the milliner's protestations that they belonged to a Scottish lodger she had turned out some while ago because he never paid any rent, Mrs Stafford and her sister were charged with witchcraft. Both women were found guilty and were publicly hanged.

One reason why the punishment handed out to Mrs Stafford and her sister was greater than that of Mother Goodridge lies in the dates when their trials took place. In 1586, Queen Elizabeth was on the throne; by 1608 James VI of Scotland had become her successor. The Elizabethan age had been fairly moderate in its attitudes to witchcraft. It is possible that Elizabeth was unwilling to condemn alleged witches to death because the majority of them were old women, but a more likely explanation for her comparative leniency is because of her friendship for Dr Dee. John Dee was a geographer and mathematician, and a favourite of Queen Elizabeth (she even made him warden of Manchester College in 1595), but he also dabbled in magic and necromancy. If the Queen had encouraged witch-hunts, her friend John Dee would have been a victim.

King James on the other hand had a terrible record of killing witches in Scotland. Under the influence of church minister James Carmichael, the King became a zealous witch-hunter. In the period 1590-97 he had 1,500 alleged witches put to death. In 1600, he even wrote a book called *Daemonologie,* telling his subjects how to recognise witches and urging them to bring witches to trial. He brought his harsh attitude with him when in 1603 he became James I of England. The Bakewell women suffered from the fact that they came to trial under his reign.

In 1619, another case where the influence of King James's witch obsession caused the death of a number of women occurred when the sixth Earl of Rutland of Haddon Hall lost his two sons, Francis and Henry. In his grief he accused six women who lived near his winter residence in Leicestershire of causing the deaths. One of the women had been a servant there until she had been dismissed for stealing food. The Earl recalled that her mother, Joan Flower, had often been suspected of being a witch, since she was ugly, swore a lot and never went to church. He had the old woman and her two daughters arrested, together with three other suspected witches. The Earl alleged that the women had stolen his sons' gloves, boiled them, pricked them, rubbed them on the back of their familiar, a cat called Rutterkin, then buried them in a manure heap. As the gloves rotted, the accusation went on, the boys had become sick and died.

Three of the women accused of killing the sons of the Earl of Rutland through witchcraft.

While in custody, and no doubt under torture, the old woman, Joan Flower, died. The authorities put out the story that she had choked to death after saying, 'If I am guilty of witchcraft, may God strike me dead!' This was proof of her guilt, and by association the guilt of the other accused women, who were all hanged.

By 1649, there was no monarch; Oliver Cromwell was Lord Protector and the Puritans were in charge. Many of the excesses of the Stuart regime were abolished but unfortunately this brought no relief for those accused of witchcraft. The new authorities of the Commonwealth period proved as cruel as their predecessors in tracking down and hanging witches. Neighbours were encouraged to report any gossip that might indicate witchcraft. And common gossip much of it was.

In 1650, Ann Wagg, a widow from Ilkeston, was accused of causing deaths through witchcraft. On 18th June, a local baker called Francis Torratt laid information before a Justice of the Peace, saying that Ann was 'commonly suspected of being a witch'. He reported that about three years earlier Ann Wagg had said bad things about him and his wife to his servant, Elizabeth Parkin. When Elizabeth had reported this to him, Ann had sought to cause her harm. The next Sunday, as Francis and his wife, together with Elizabeth Parkin, were going to church, Ann Wagg had stood in their way. She frowned at Elizabeth, but spoke no words. That same night Elizabeth had fallen sick and was unable to 'go a stone's cast'. Francis had the maid sleep on a bed close to him and his wife, but at nine o'clock, they heard her cry out. Francis said that neither he nor his wife were able to speak or move until they saw something jump from Elizabeth's bed. The maid called out that it was a cat and told them to watch where it went. Once the cat had gone, Francis found that he and his wife could move and speak again. Ann Wagg was known to have a cat, not just a pet but a familiar that sucked blood from her and brought her messages from the Devil. Torratt also alleged that Ann Wagg had caused the minister's wife to fall ill.

It was believed that one method of immobilising a witch

was to thrust a pair of tongs into the fire and she would be powerless until they were withdrawn. This had been tried on Ann Wagg and it was seen that she could not move until the tongs were withdrawn from the fire. Proof indeed that Ann was a witch!

Other witnesses gave evidence to the same Justice, Gervase Bennet, Esquire. William Smith, a husbandman, stated that two months earlier Ann Wagg had come to obtain milk, and being refused she went away grumbling. The next morning they found a calf of theirs dead, although it had been well overnight. Alice Carpenter said that Ann Wagg was of ill repute, and that about 12 months ago Alice's child was taken with a shrieking and foaming at the mouth. The child so continued for about a week, and then died.

Not all the evidence was first hand. Alice Day reported that two or three years earlier one Elizabeth Webster died 'who took upon her death that Ann Wagg had done her hurt.' Neither was the evidence all from recent years. Elizabeth Gothard said that about 15 years ago Ann Wagg came to her house to buy wheat but Elizabeth told her that the wheat was promised to her sister. Ann had grumbled and said, 'Is not my money as good as hers?' The same night, Elizabeth's daughter fell ill, taken with a continual shaking. She continued to shake for a week and then recovered. Then the same Ann Wagg came a fortnight later to buy butter, but Elizabeth having none for her she went away. That very same night the child fell sick again and this time she died.

The tendency of people to accuse others of being witches might be thought to have died out centuries ago, but in February 2003 posters appeared on walls in the south Derbyshire town of Swadlincote, naming three local women and accusing them of witchcraft. The poster advised the 'good people of Swad' to guard against the trio who will 'cast a spell on anyone who crosses their path.' One of the victims, whose address and telephone number were on the poster, had no option but to report the matter to the police. Just as in the days of Mother Goodridge and Ann Wagg, the accusation of being a witch is still an easy way for spiteful townsfolk to seek revenge for some imagined wrong.

Another recent manifestation of this traditional fear of witchcraft occurred in Stretton where a local theatre company was putting on a performance of Roald Dahl's children's story *The Witches*. The very name of the play was enough to trigger opposition. The hall where the play was to be performed was broken into, and vandalised. The perpetrators left a written message warning the drama group to steer away from witchcraft and to return to Christianity.

THE FRAMING OF
ALICE WHEELDON

———————— ✿ ————————

To say that fifty year old Alice Wheeldon was a radical thinker would be an understatement. She was a feminist and a supporter of the women's suffrage movement, although she found its leaders disappointingly half-hearted. She was an ardent socialist, a convinced atheist and, above all, a committed pacifist. She was completely opposed to the war that had broken out in 1914 and was extremely proud of her son William who was being held in prison as a conscientious objector. Her attitude to the war contrasted with many of the leaders of the suffrage movement, who supported the war and even gave out white feathers to young men who failed to serve in the army.

Alice lived at 12 Pear Tree Road, Derby, the front of her house being a shop where she sold secondhand clothes. There is evidence that, as well as being a shopkeeper, she had also taught in elementary schools. Living with her was her daughter Harriet, known as Hetty, who was – surprisingly – a scripture teacher. Given both women's professed atheism, Hetty's scripture lessons must have been unusually interesting. Another daughter, Winifred, was married to Alfred Mason, a college laboratory assistant in Southampton.

The Wheeldon family was opposed to conscription, and the house in Pear Tree Road often sheltered conscientious objectors and army deserters on the run. One further resident was a lodger calling himself Alec Gordon. Alec claimed to be a fugitive from military service, and as such he was warmly welcomed into the household. However, Alice and Harriet were being too trusting: 'Alec' was in fact a

Pear Tree Road in 1916, the location of Alice Wheedon's home and shop. (Derby Telegraph)

government agent named Mr E. Vivian who had been sent to infiltrate the Wheeldon family. He introduced Alice to another man, known as Comrade Bert, supposedly an army deserter and a member of the IWW (the International Workers of the World). But Bert, like Alec Gordon, was not what he seemed.

However, to the trusting Derby women, Alec and Bert were both committed to the causes of pacifism and socialism, giving valuable advice and support to various projects. One of these was a plan to break into a prison camp where conscientious objectors were being held. Pointing out that the camp had fierce guard dogs, Alec said that it would be necessary to poison the dogs before the prisoners could be rescued. Alice agreed, and wrote to her son-in-law in Southampton to ask if he could obtain strychnine and curare, which, she was told, would be suitable poisons for the task. Animal Welfare seems to be the only radical cause that was not espoused by Alice Wheeldon, though it may be that she regarded the death of the guard dogs as the unpleasant but necessary price to be paid for the freeing of men wrongly imprisoned.

Alfred and Winifred Mason shared Alice's views, and Alfred managed to obtain the two poisons from the laboratory at Hartley University College where he worked. In January 1917, four phials of strychnine and curare were dispatched from Alfred's home in Southampton to the Wheeldon house in Derby.

The police immediately raided the homes of the Wheeldons and the Masons and arrested the four family members: Alice and Harriet in Derby and Alfred and Winifred in Southampton. They were charged with conspiring to murder the Prime Minister, David Lloyd George, and his minister Arthur Henderson. It was alleged that the poisons were to be used on darts to be thrown or fired at the two leading politicians.

The prosecution was led by Sir Frederick ('F.E.') Smith, the Attorney General, and the only witness was 'Comrade Bert', now revealed to be Herbert Booth, a government agent working for an intelligence section within the Ministry of Munitions, a department which later became part of MI5 and the Special Branch.

According to Booth, the four accused were hardened political terrorists who had previously tried to kill the Chancellor of the Exchequer in 1915 by sending him a poisoned needle through the post. Just for good measure, he mentioned that they were violent atheists who had once burned down a church at Breadsall, a village to the north of Derby. He claimed that Alice had told him of a previous plot by members of the women's suffrage movement who had spent £300 in an attempt to kill Lloyd George by getting into a hotel where he was staying and driving a nail tipped with poison through the sole of his boot.

Alice, like her fellow accused, pleaded not guilty, and explained that the poison was to be used to kill guard dogs in a project to free prisoners whose only crime was to oppose the war. Her story was not believed, however, and three of the four accused were found guilty of conspiracy to assassinate the Prime Minister. The exception was Harriet Wheeldon, who was freed. Alice was sentenced to ten years in prison, Alfred Mason to seven years and Winifred to five years. The judge said that Winifred's sentence was lighter because she had obviously been influenced by her wicked mother.

The accused were never likely to win their case. The prosecution team led by the Attorney General included two KCs, a junior barrister, and dozens of expert witnesses, including leading pathologist Bernard Spilsbury. The defence consisted of only one barrister, Mr Riza, and one solicitor. Mr Riza, said to be related to the Persian royal family, seems to have been somewhat eccentric in his approach to law, demanding at one point that his clients should undergo Trial By Ordeal. This was a reference to the medieval practice of accused prisoners proving their innocence by walking over hot coals, with the Almighty protecting the innocent from harm. It was a ludicrous suggestion, not least to the firmly non-religious Wheeldons.

Riza did, however, make the very telling important point that, although 'Comrade Bert' gave evidence, the Crown refused to produce the mysterious 'Alec Gordon', presumably the more senior of the agents. This meant that the defence was unable to question him about his role in the plot to obtain the strychnine and curare.

Alice had sent several letters to her son-in-law on the subject of obtaining poisons. Most of the letters stated clearly that the poisons were for killing guard dogs but the only letters produced in court were ones where dogs were not specifically mentioned.

The judge, Mr Justice Low, made much of the fact that Alice and her daughters had often used obscenities when talking about the Prime Minister and other government figures. He commented on their foul language, saying that since they had both been teachers, then it obviously followed that elementary education was not a good idea. The prosecution frequently asked questions which led Alice to agree that she regarded Arthur Henderson as a traitor to the working class, that she hated Lloyd George and that she thought it would be a good thing if his career came to an end. She admitted once saying that 'George of Buckingham Palace' was another man who deserved to be done in, though she added that she had only said it 'at that time in my bitterness.'

The whole trial was one-sided, and it is not surprising that the jury took only thirty minutes to reach its verdict. The whole atmosphere of wartime Britain was one of suspicion and rumour. German spies were seen everywhere. A trial in 1916 was interrupted when a *Times* reporter was accused of taking notes in German writing, though it later turned out that he was using an old form of shorthand. A pro-German organisation known as the Hidden Hand was said to be sapping the fighting spirit of the British forces by spreading lesbianism and homosexuality.

This atmosphere, plus the fact that every town in England had lost husbands and sons in the desperate massacres of the trenches, meant that the trial of the Wheeldon family was not going to be even-handed.

After the trial was over, but before the court dispersed, the judge gave permission for Mrs Emmeline Pankhurst, the women's suffrage leader, to make a statement. In it, Mrs Pankhurst stated that the Women's Political and Social Union had never offered money for an attempt on the life of Lloyd George, and would never countenance the taking of any human life. Edward Garner, in his book *Was You Ever In Dovedale?*, takes the view that this statement might have been useful to Alice Wheeldon's case and should have been heard earlier, during the trial.

It seems to me that Alice Wheeldon, about to start a ten-year sentence, might have heard the words of the statement with some cynicism. She was already disillusioned with the way that the suffragists' leaders had ceased their political activities to support the war. Now, here was Mrs Pankhurst come to denounce the more radical of the feminist activitists, those who opposed the war.

The trial, held at the Old Bailey, was a national sensation at the time, but it is now widely accepted that there was no plot to assassinate David Lloyd George. The authorities were anxious to discredit those who were providing underground help for conscientious objectors to evade imprisonment, and sent in two spies – Herbert Booth and the more shadowy E. Vivian – to first infiltrate and then subvert the Wheeldons' activities. It is probable that the first idea of obtaining poison came from one of these two agents. It is certain that its use was to be for poisoning guard dogs, and that the fantastic plot to assassinate Lloyd George was a fiction devised by shadowy secret service forces.

It is possible that Lloyd George realised this, because after the war was over, he had Alice Wheeldon, together with her daughter and son-in-law, released from prison. On his express orders a Home Office review was held in 1919, and it was decided that the three had been convicted on dubious evidence. Although Alice was released, she had been so weakened by her treatment in prison – including hard labour and force-feeding during hunger strikes – that she died a few weeks after her release. She was buried in an unmarked grave in Derby's Nottingham Road cemetery.

Alec Gordon, the government spy and probable *agent provocateur*, emigrated to South Africa in an uncanny replica of the final destination of Oliver the spy (see Chapter 3), in the case of the Pentrich Rising a hundred years earlier.

If the authorities' original intention was to silence Alice Wheeldon and to wipe out all public memory of her existence and her ideals, it is pleasing to note that they failed. *A Plot To Kill Lloyd George*, a BBC television programme broadcast in 1983, investigated the events of 1916-17, with Brenda Bruce recreating the role of Alice Wheeldon. This programme came to the conclusion that there *was* a conspiracy, but it was one to frame the Wheeldons, rather than one to assassinate the Prime Minister. In 1988, the case was recreated on the stage in a play called *The Friends of Alice Wheeldon* by Sheila Rowbotham.

PHANTOM PLANES OF
THE DARK PEAK

❀

There have been many sightings of mysterious planes flying over the Dark Peak area of north Derbyshire. Some of these mystery planes have been explained away as light aircraft involved in clandestine and nefarious activities. Both drug smuggling and arms transactions have been alleged. But some of the sightings have involved ghostly Lancaster bombers and Dakotas, dating from the 1940s, flying silently over the high moors.

The name the Dark Peak, like that of the Peak District as a whole, is rather misleading, since there are no mountain peaks there, just miles of high moorland plateau.

It is perhaps not surprising that people should look for ghostly aircraft in the area since over fifty planes have crashed there since 1945, with a loss of over three hundred lives, and debris from some of these crashes is still there, lying scattered on the moors. In May 1945, a Lancaster bomber of the Royal Canadian 408 Squadron crashed on Bleaklow. Two months later, an American Dakota crashed in the same area. In November 1948, a photographic recognisance aircraft – probably an RB-29A or an F-13A – crashed with the pilot Landon P. Tanner and his crew losing their lives. In August 1949, a Dakota piloted by Captain Frank Pinkerton crashed near Kinder Intake, killing twenty-one of its crew and passengers.

The crashes were not confined to the 1940s, but are still occurring. In 1993, a storm caused a private Jet – a Hawker Hunter – to crash. This plane, with its pilot Wallace Cubitt, was never found and it is believed to lie thirty feet below the peat bog of Broomhead Moor.

Among the local people who have seen ghostly phantoms connected with these crashed planes is Tony Ingle, a retired postman. In April 1995, Tony was staying at a caravan site near the village of Hope. He was out walking his golden retriever, when he became aware of the dark shadow of a large plane passing over him. Tony says that the plane was flying only sixty feet above him and it temporarily blocked out the sun. The plane banked and appeared to come down sharply into a field behind a hedge. When Tony ran to the field there was nothing there but quietly grazing sheep. It was as if nothing untoward had happened, but Tony's dog Ben now refuses to go along the lane where they were when the incident occurred, or into the field where the plane appeared to crash. The strangest aspect of the phenomenon is that although the plane was low enough for Tony to see its propellers turning, he could hear no sound at all. Tony told the press, 'I don't believe in ghosts and I have wracked my brains for a logical explanation but I can't find one.' He is sure the plane involved was a Dakota. A phantom Dakota was also seen by rambler John O'Neill while he was walking in the local hills.

Ron Collier, an aviation historian who has written two books about the aircraft wrecks of the Dark Peak, believes that there has to be some rational explanation, but admits to sensing a force governing the moors. He points out that many of the people who have seen the phantom planes are plain-speaking farmers who are too sensible to believe in ghost stories. 'Something is going on,' he concludes, 'but it is very difficult to explain what it is.'

People sometimes indulge in the ghoulish habit of going to the crash sites to remove pieces of aircraft debris as souvenirs. It is mainly non-local visitors to the area who commit this disrespectful act, but one peakland farmer admits that he did once take some plane parts back to his farm, hoping to find some use for them. He stored them in his barn, but when his son reported seeing the barn shaking violently for no apparent reason, the repentant souvenir-hunter decided to return the pieces of the aeroplane to the crash site. After his act of penitence, the barn became a stable structure once more, and gave no further trouble.

In 1982, Helen and David Shaw were travelling past the Ladybower Reservoir and pulled up for a moment. It was a bright October night, and they were amazed to see a World War II Lancaster bomber flying over the water towards them. The plane was only four hundred yards away and they could observe it quite clearly. Another local couple who have seen the plane, describing it as 'a big old grey war plane' were Steven and Barbara Morgan. They said the plane headed into the hillside but they heard no crash.

One of the strangest events – or series of events – took place shortly after 10 pm on the evening of Monday 24th March 1997, on Howden Moor. This moor lies north of the Howden, Derwent and Ladybower reservoirs, and is half in north Derbyshire, half in south Yorkshire. A number of people had gone out on the moors to watch for the Hale-Bopp comet but what they saw instead was a propeller-driven plane flying low overhead. The plane seemed to be in difficulty, and the witnesses were sure that it had come down. Gamekeeper Mike Ellison and his wife Barbara heard a terrific explosion in the Strines area of the moor.

Steve Tattersfield, himself a pilot, and his wife Marie-France Tattersfield, a special constable, were driving near the village of Bolsterstone when they saw what appeared to be a four-seater aircraft flying west towards Broomhead Moor. The windows on the plane were brightly lit, and it was very low, no higher than five hundred feet, well below the legal night-time altitude. The plane disappeared behind some tall conifers.

Mr Morton, a farmer from Bolsterstone, also saw a low-flying plane travelling at what seemed to him a low speed. Soon afterwards he and his mother saw an orange glow and smoke, and noticed a strong burning smell. John Littlewood, a gamekeeper, was out on Midhope Moor when he saw the plane. He described it as an old-time plane, but definitely not a Lancaster or a Hercules. He too estimated the altitude of the plane at five hundred feet and said that it was 'long, slow and low'.

Many of the witnesses dialled 999 to report the crash, and the emergency services of four counties took part in a massive search for what was believed to be a major air disaster. Two helicopters, a hundred and fifty mountain rescue workers, and a hundred police officers with tracker dogs took part in a search that lasted for fifteen hours, at an estimated cost of £50,000. But no trace of a plane was ever found, and no planes were ever reported missing.

A detailed account of the events on Howden Moor can be found in an internet article by David Clarke and Martin Jeffrey at www.flyingsaucery.com. These two researchers give particulars of the many strange sightings of that evening, how some ufologists have concluded that an RAF plane was shot down by alien craft, and how questions came to be asked in Parliament.

The area round the Derwent and Howden dams has been connected with tales of phantom planes for about fifty years. These date back to the time when Wing Commander Guy Gibson and his 617 Squadron were practising with the so-called 'bouncing bomb' to be used in the Dambusters raids on the German dams at Eder and Moehne. The bouncing bomb was, in fact, a backwardly-rotating depth charge. Derbyshire-born Dr Barnes Wallis established that if the depth charge was released from an aircraft at a carefully calculated point, at the right speed, at the right altitude and the right distance from the dam, it would skim over the water until it reached the dam wall. There it would sink to a predetermined depth before exploding and breaking the dam below water level. Anyone who has played Ducks and Drakes as a child will know how a flat stone can be made to skip over water for a considerable distance, bouncing a number of times. With the bouncing bombs, the plan was to make a depth charge weighing over nine thousand pounds do the same thing before sinking and exploding!

The pilots who were to take part in the Dambusters raids needed to practise these skills, and two of the places used were the Derwent and Howden dams. Although other areas were used for practice as well, the Derbyshire dams were particularly useful because their twin towers replicated the

The twin towers of Derwent Dam used for aiming practice by the Dambusters Squadron. (David Moorley)

towers on the German target dams. The airmen were able to use a triangular device, which they sighted on the towers to tell them when to release their bouncing bombs. It is known that Guy Gibson practised on the Derwent Reservoir in March and April 1943, in a Lancaster bomber, accompanied by Squadron Leader Young and Flight Lieutenant Hopgood, both of whom lost their lives in the Dambusters raids in May 1943.

Given this local connection, it is not surprising that so many of the phantom planes seen flying over north Derbyshire are said to be Lancaster bombers, though it should be noted that no Lancasters were lost while the 617 Squadron was practising in Derbyshire.

Another location in the Derbyshire Dark Peak area where mysterious phenomena have been regularly seen is in the Longdendale valley, near Glossop. Here the sightings are of mysterious lights on the moorlands, and unlike the phantom planes, these have been recorded for centuries. On several occasions, members of the Mountain Rescue team have been called out, as the lights have been interpreted as those of lost ramblers or climbers. These have been described as a string of moving lights that eventually fade, and it is easy to see how these appear to belong to lost walkers. On other occasions, however, there appears to be a single beam like a searchlight, and, not surprisingly, these lights have been claimed by ufologists, who believe that they are evidence of alien craft visiting Earth.

The older sightings of wandering lights were once believed to have been caused by lanterns carried by hobs or fairy folk, though today people wonder if they are an unexplained but entirely natural phenomenon.

WHO KILLED
WENDY SEWELL?

---------❀---------

Bakewell, in north-west Derbyshire, is a small market town, famous for its local delicacy the Bakewell pudding, always known outside Derbyshire as 'the Bakewell tart'. I grew up in a similar market town in Leicestershire, and well remember that my town was 'run' by a number of local men – businessmen, shopkeepers, solicitors and farmers. We always referred to them as 'the forty thieves'. Bakewell in the sixties and early seventies was much the same, though being a smaller town there were probably fewer than forty of them. What would have been very similar was the fact that anyone from a working class background, especially some-one from a council estate, did not get the same respect as one of the ruling cabal. We didn't think there was anything wrong with this; it was the way things were.

It was in this atmosphere that Stephen Downing grew up. Stephen did not shine at school, and when he left the local C of E Boys' School at sixteen, he had a reading age of only eleven. He lived at home with his parents, Ray and Nita, and his younger sister Christine in a council house in Bakewell. He was known on the estate as a kind and caring boy, who would willingly help others. He had his faults, of course, including a disinclination to leave his bed in the mornings. The only other negative comment heard locally was that he was a bit daft, the local Derbyshire term for anyone who was naïve or of low IQ. He was passive, gentle and a bit lazy.

His first job after leaving school was at the local bakers called Bloomers, who ran a café and shop in the town centre. At Bloomers, Stephen caused consternation and amusement in equal measure when he made humorous gingerbread men (and women) whose gender was rather evident! His colleagues obviously did not find this too offensive as the creations were displayed in the shop window, until head office heard about it. On the positive side, he designed and made a beautiful bread wheatsheaf that was used as the centrepiece at the church harvest festival, a source of much pride to Stephen and his parents.

However, Stephen was often late for work and this led to him losing his job the following year. After a few days as a plasterer, and a few months at an engineering works, Stephen found work with Bakewell Urban District Council as a gardener in the local cemetery. He had worked there for about seven months when an event occurred which was to shatter his life. It was 12th September 1973, a frosty Wednesday morning. Ray Downing rose at 5.30 am, and went off to his job as a bus driver. Nita called Stephen at 7.20 am to see if he was going into work, as he had been off with a cold the previous two days. He stumbled down at the last minute, late as usual, getting dressed in such a hurry that he put his best boots on, instead of his work ones. He set off for work, only a few minutes' walk away.

Nita got home from work just after 1 pm, and she had only just put the kettle on when she heard Stephen come in. He changed his boots, and asked his mum if she could buy him a bottle of pop from the shop and bring it down to the cemetery for him. He said he had been unable to buy the pop himself as the shop was already closed for dinner. He left the money for the pop, along with the empty bottle to return. In those days, you received a small sum of money from the shop when you took the bottle back.

Stephen went back to the cemetery and immediately made a terrible discovery. Lying face down on the cemetery footpath was a badly battered young woman. Stephen knelt beside her and turned her over. When the woman sat up and shook her head, splattering him with drops of blood, he went for help. Having no money for the public phone box, he headed for the lodge where the cemetery keeper, Wilf Walker, lived. The two of them hurried to the spot where the young woman was lying injured, though she was now yards

Stephen Downing served 27 years for the murder but the conviction was ruled unsafe. (Derby Telegraph)

from where Stephen had found her. She tried to get up again, then fell back against the gravestone. Four other workmen came over to see what was happening, and one was sent to phone for the police. One of the men, Herbert Dawson, was later to tell the court that he saw a person lying on the graves, trying to wipe blood from their eyes with the back of a hand. The person, now recognisable as a woman, tried to stand up but fell again.

When a police officer, PC Ball, arrived, he told everyone not to touch anything. Stephen Downing said that he had touched the woman, to turn her over, when he first found her. It was noticeable that Stephen had blood on his trouser knees. There was a bloodstained pickaxe handle nearby, and Stephen said that it must have come from the workman's store in the disused chapel. Stephen had blood on his hands and asked if he could wash them. The officer said that he should not, but bizarrely he did allow Stephen to go and help the other men to load asbestos sheets from the chapel-cum-store into a van.

Forty minutes after Stephen Downing first found the injured woman, an ambulance arrived to take her to hospital. While she was being helped at the scene, the woman tried to push away her helpers, and during the journey in the ambulance, she was very restless and threw her right arm about. When she arrived at Chesterfield Royal Hospital, she was found to have multiple lacerations of the skull, and x-rays confirmed that the skull was fractured in a number of places.

The young woman, now identified as thirty-three year old Mrs Wendy Sewell, died two days later. At the post mortem, the pathologist found that she had fifteen skull lacerations, probably caused by blows from the pickaxe shaft. He concluded that she had received seven or eight violent blows from someone in a frenzied state. Her shoulder was dislocated, possibly in a struggle with her attacker. There was no evidence of sexual interference.

As the ambulance had arrived at the cemetery, Stephen Downing was being taken to the police station for question-ing. In a manner that would be illegal today and was unprofessional even then, Stephen was questioned almost continually for nine hours. He was not cautioned or allowed to see a solicitor or his family, and at times he had to be shaken to stay awake. He was cold, tired, hungry and frightened. He was also suffering from a pain in his back, which later proved to be an abscess at the base of his spine. The officers kept putting to him that he had assaulted Mrs Sewell himself, before leaving the cemetery to go to the shop. Officers told him that they knew he had done it and that he would be questioned all night if necessary. One added that he would bet a week's wages that Stephen would admit it in the end. Belatedly, at 10.30 pm, Stephen was cautioned, and at about 11 pm he agreed to confess, hoping that he would be allowed to rest. Unaware that Wendy Sewell's injuries would prove to be fatal, Stephen was fairly sure that when she came round she would tell the police the true identity of her attacker.

Asked to make a statement, and ashamed of his lack of writing and reading skills, the naïve youth agreed that the police should actually write it from his spoken account. Stephen remembers that from time to time they suggested 'better' wording. In one example, when he said that he watched the woman, one officer said it would read better if he said he followed her with his eyes. When they read the statement back to him, he realised that they had written that he had followed the woman. Stephen objected but was told that following her meant much the same as watching her. When the statement was complete, Stephen was asked to sign it in biro, though the statement itself was written in pencil.

The statement itself, as later produced in court, read: *I don't know what made me do it. I saw this woman walking in the cemetery. I went into the chapel to get the pickaxe handle that I knew was there. I followed her but I hadn't talked to her and she hadn't talked to me, but I think she knew I was there. I came right up to her near enough. I hit her twice on the head, on the back of the neck. I just hit her at the back of the neck to knock her out. She fell to the ground and she was on her side, and then she was face*

*down. I rolled her over and started to undress her. I pulled
her bra off first. I had to pull her jumper up and I just got
hold of it until it broke, and then I pulled her pants and her
knickers off. I started to play with her breasts and then her
vagina. I put my middle finger up her vagina. I don't know
why I hit her but it might have been to do with what I have
just told you. But I knew I had to knock her out first before
I did anything to her. It was only a couple of minutes. I was
playing with her and there was just a bit of blood at the back
of her neck. So I left her, went back to the chapel, got my
pop bottle and went to the shop, and then went home to see
my mother and asked her to get a bottle of pop for me
because the shop was shut. I suppose I did that so that no
one would find out I'd hit the woman. I went back to the
cemetery about fifteen minutes later and went back to see
the woman. She was lying on the ground the same way as I'd
left her but she was covered in blood on her face and on her
back. I bent down to see how she was and she was semi-
conscious, just. She put her hands up to her face and just
kept wiping her face with her hand. She had been doing that
when I first knocked her down. I went back to the telephone
kiosk to ring for the police and ambulance so they would
think someone else had done it and I'd just found her. I
hadn't any money so I went to the Lodge and asked Wilf
Walker if he was on the telephone, but he said he wasn't. So
I told him what I'd supposed to have found. He came to
have a look and then he went to ask these other blokes in a
white van outside the cemetery if they had seen her, but they
said they hadn't, so one of them went to phone for the
police. I just stayed because there was no place to go.*

It is hard to see how someone with a reading age of eleven
would have used words like *semi-conscious* and *vagina*.
Indeed the judge at Stephen Downing's trial was to comment
on the latter usage, as well as pointing out that the prosecution must establish that the confession was voluntarily made
and no oppression used.

The other very noticeable factor about the confession is
where Stephen admits to striking Wendy Sewell twice. The
police who were questioning him had, at this time, no idea

that the pathologist would conclude that she had been struck seven or eight times. It may be cynical to conclude that, had they known, the confession would have said that Stephen had struck an unspecified number of blows. Stephen now says that he picked the number two completely at random. The pathologist also stated that the person who had struck the blows had done so in a frenzy. Although PC Ball was later to state that when he arrived at the scene Stephen Downing seemed excited, everyone else present – Wilf Walker and the four workmen – said that he seemed perfectly calm and normal.

Thirteen days after making the statement, Stephen Downing retracted it, saying that it was untrue.

Despite the retraction, Stephen's confession formed the main plank of the prosecution case at his trial for murder the following February. It was alleged that Stephen attacked Wendy Sewell before leaving the cemetery to return home at lunchtime. He then returned and reported finding the injured woman. Despite the fact that a witness, Mrs Louisa Hadfield, gave evidence that she saw a young man, fair-haired and about six feet tall, running away from the cemetery area at 1.15 pm on the day of the murder, the jury took only an hour to return a verdict of guilty. The judge, Mr Justice Nield, sentenced the slow-witted seventeen year old youth to be detained 'at Her Majesty's Pleasure'. This phrase, necessary because Stephen was under eighteen, meant that his imprisonment could be reviewed at any time but it was recommended that he would serve seventeen years.

Stephen's father campaigned tirelessly for his son's release, and an appeal was held in October, eight months after the trial. At this hearing a fifteen year old witness, Jayne Atkins, said that she had seen Wendy Sewell and a man with their arms around each other on the day Wendy was attacked. Her evidence was judged not credible because she had not come forward at the time of the trial, although the girl explained this by saying she was afraid the man had seen her and might come after her. The police commented that although they believed the girl, they thought she had seen the couple on a different day. This ignores the fact that 12th September was the first day of school, and Jayne was wearing her school uniform. If she had seen them on an earlier date then she would not have been wearing those clothes. Nevertheless her evidence was dismissed, and Stephen remained in prison. After Jayne had appeared at the appeal hearing, her family received anonymous threats and left Bakewell to live in a town fifty miles away.

Ray and Nita continued to try to prove their son's innocence, even employing the services of a private investigator. However, a second appeal held in 1981 was equally unsuccessful.

Stephen was not released when he had served seventeen years. Although all the reports on him said that he was 'polite, courteous and co-operative', 'friendly and communicative to both staff and inmates', and 'his attitude towards women has been commendable', his release was always refused on the ground that he was in denial of guilt. This meant that despite being categorised as being no danger to the public Stephen could not be considered for release while he continued to say that he had not committed the murder of Wendy Sewell.

He had already been in prison for twenty years when, in 1994, Ray Downing approached Don Hale, the editor of the *Matlock Mercury*, to ask for his help. Don had been a young professional footballer in Lancashire before becoming a sports reporter. He had been a full-time reporter on local radio, then news editor of the *Bury Messenger*, subsequently taking up the post as editor of the local paper in Matlock, some eight miles from Bakewell. His journalistic experience was to become very important, together with his tremendous determination and a vast amount of moral and physical courage.

Don was initially cautious about getting involved but as he examined the circumstances of the attack on Wendy Sewell and the way the police had put together the case against Stephen Downing, he became convinced that further investigation was justified. As he dug deeper, the more his personal courage was needed. He received the first threatening phone call immediately after his initial visit to Ray Downing's house in Bakewell, long before anything was published in his newspaper. That call simply told him to keep his nose out of the case, but later calls were to threaten violence and even death. The offices of the *Matlock Mercury* were attacked, and pressure was applied on the advertising revenue of the paper. There were also three violent attacks on Don himself, two of them involving attempted hit-and-run 'accidents'. The third attempt on his life took place in April 1995 when he was driving on the A515 one evening, having been falsely tipped off about a farm fire. A huge quarry truck came up close behind him and began to blare its horn before repeatedly bumping into the back of his car. When Don managed to pull into a layby and to turn his car round, the truck also turned and pursued him again. The nightmare scenario, like a scene from the film *Duel*, reached a climax when Don saw another huge lorry parked across the road. He drove off the road through a field gate and the two heavy trucks collided.

So what had the journalist done to cause this violent reaction?

He had discovered that Wendy Sewell had enjoyed a full and varied love life. Among her lovers were a number of local businessmen and farmers, all from the group of prominent Bakewell people. This information, along with the location, led some tabloids to call her by the name of the Bakewell delicacy mentioned in the opening paragraph. This label – and Don Hale never fell into this usage – is unfair. We are talking about the late sixties and early seventies, a hedonistic period after the discovery of the contraceptive pill and well before the onset of AIDS.

He had discovered that other people besides Jayne Atkins and Mrs Hadfield had seen various men behaving strangely at or just after the murder in the vicinity of Bakewell cemetery. Three young children had been terrified when a bloodstained man had leapt over the cemetery wall where they were playing. Other witnesses spoke of seeing a man in an orange tee-shirt hanging about the cemetery just before the attack. Everyone who reported their evidence to the police said that they had not been taken seriously, being told that 'we've already got someone in custody.'

He discovered that one policeman had told many people, including Wendy Sewell's husband, that the youth in custody was a known pervert, which was completely untrue. He discovered that one of Wendy's ex-lovers had concocted a false alibi for himself, and had been driven into Bakewell that day. He discovered that Wendy had been visited by a man shortly before leaving her place of work at about 12.25 pm.

Don Hale's investigations met a continual stone wall of silence from the authorities. He was astounded to be told that all the papers connected with the case, and the bloodstained murder weapon, had been destroyed. The official silence contrasted with the many ordinary Bakewell people who told him that they had always known that the convicted young gardener was not guilty. Everyone had a theory about the identity of the real killers, but were frightened of upsetting the Bakewell cabal.

Because of the obstruction that he met, it was a further seven years before Don's researches had the desired effect of getting Stephen Downing released. After twenty-seven years in prison, the appeal court finally agreed that his confession was obtained in a manner that made the conviction unsafe. The police officers who had questioned him were said to have committed substantial and significant breaches of the rules on interrogating suspects. Many of Stephen's supporters thought that the evidence proved Stephen not guilty of the crime and were disappointed that the appeal court did not proclaim his innocence. He was released in January 2002.

Don Hale's campaigning journalism and personal courage led to him receiving fifteen national and international awards, including Journalist of the Year and Man of the Year. He was awarded the OBE for his services to campaigning journalism. His book *Town Without Pity*, written in collaboration with husband and wife team Marika Huns and Hamish McGregor, was nominated for the Crime Writers' Association dagger for non-fiction in 2002. It is essential reading for anyone with an interest in Derbyshire, police procedures, campaigning for justice, or crime in general. Ironically, the book written by the man some Derbyshire police officers used to call 'that mad bugger from Matlock' became required reading for those officers who had to reinvestigate Wendy Sewell's murder.

So who did kill Wendy Sewell?

One possibility that has to be considered is that Stephen Downing really did do it. One person who now supports this theory is Christine Smith, a professional medium who joined Don Hale's campaign, claiming initially that in Bakewell cemetery she had experienced a psychic feeling of Wendy Sewell undressing, then being attacked by a man she already knew. Over the years, Christine visited Stephen Downing in prison and formed a close relationship with him after his release. However, in May 2002, she produced a tape recording of Stephen saying that he had committed the murder. This led to headlines in the *Daily Telegraph* which read 'I Feared For My Safety, Says "Bakewell Tape" Woman'. Stephen's comment was that he felt betrayed by a woman he thought loved him. 'She was on and on at me,' he explained, 'and she rang me up saying that she had had a psychic vision of me doing the killing. Eventually, I just blurted out that if it made her happy, okay then I did it. I said it to see how she would react. I was stupid but I just wanted to test her love for me.' It was this telephone conversation that was being recorded.

This event did give succour to those who were always reluctant to accept Stephen's innocence. One retired police inspector, not from the Derbyshire force, stated to me, 'Well, he's confessed at least twice now. What more do you want?'

After a six months' reinvestigation of the case, the Derbyshire police announced in February 2003 that they had checked out twenty-two possible suspects in the case, and had found no evidence against them. The report concluded: 'The police are not looking for any other person for the murder of Wendy Sewell. All possible lines of enquiry have been exhausted. The case is now closed.' In their own words, 'Stephen Downing remains our only suspect.'

This report led one national tabloid newspaper – not a normal supporter of liberal causes – to comment: 'What are the police trying to do to Stephen Downing? Yesterday, Derbyshire police played judge and jury and tried him again at a press conference. What purpose is served by the police branding him again? It smacks of getting their own back.'

To accept the police version of events means believing that Stephen committed a frenzied murder, then calmly went home to see his mum and change his boots. It also means believing that he chose to spend twenty-seven years in prison when he could have done ten years less simply by stating his guilt. And why would Don Hale have been threatened and attacked, if the real culprit wasn't frightened of what he might find out?

It still seems far more likely that the crime was committed either by someone Wendy knew, perhaps after a lover's quarrel or in a fit of jealousy, or by someone acting on his behalf. It is also possible that more than one man was present at the murder, and that neither of them was Stephen Downing.

THE MYSTERY OF
ABBOR LOW

———————————————— ❀ ————————————————

Arbor Low, sometimes known as 'the Stonehenge of the
north', is situated on Middleton Moor, some 1,000 feet
above sea level. It dates back to 2500 BC and consists of
forty-six huge limestone slabs, and thirteen smaller ones,
arranged in a circle with one group in the centre. The whole
henge is surrounded by a raised earthwork and a five foot
ditch. Unlike the Wiltshire Stonehenge, the stones at Arbor
Low all lie flat. There is some debate about the reason for
this. Some claim that they have fallen after centuries of
strong Derbyshire winds, but another school postulates that
the early Christians pushed them over to destroy their pagan
power. Currently, the most widely accepted theory is that the
stones were always meant to lie horizontally on the earth.

The name Arbor Low may provide a clue. The word Low
(or Lowe) is common in Derbyshire and neighbouring
counties, and denotes a burial mound. The word Arbor has
no connection with arbour and trees, but is a very old word
meaning an axle or spindle. Seen from above, the stones do
resemble a wheel, though others have said they look like a
clockface. The wheel theory, however, would tie in with
'axle'.

Visiting Arbor Low on the last day of April 2003, the first
thing that struck me was how isolated the place was. No
brown tourist signs pointing the way, no road signs of any
kind until you reach the actual farm track that leads to the
henge. It is almost as if the visitor is not meant to find it.
Perhaps making it difficult to find cuts out the casual
daytripper and helps to maintain the sense of secrecy and
mystery. I went there with David Moorley who joined me in

order to take photographs and we were the only people at Arbor Low that morning, though another car was arriving as we left. Well, we were the only human visitors there. We did have one other companion: the farm collie that greeted us as we got out of the car accompanied us through the farmyard, and preceded us up onto Arbor Low. The dog only deserted us when he spotted the other car coming up the farm track and rushed to go through his performance again.

David, the farm dog and I had the strange mysterious location, with its magnificent views of the surrounding Derbyshire countryside, to ourselves. It was extremely atmospheric, not melancholy or desolate, but with a feeling of power that must date back over four and a half thousand years. Many believe Arbor Low to be a place of supernatural force. Wayne Anthony, in his book *Haunted Derbyshire*, says that Arbor Low has for centuries been a place of strange occurrences and ghostly sightings. W. M. Turner, author of *Romances of the Peak*, describes meeting a young shepherd on a visit to Arbor Low in 1895 and being told that no one would visit the location at night for fear of boggarts or hobgoblins. It was commonly held that people were buried there, and some thought there might have been a great battle. The battle is probably an oral tale that has little historical basis, and the notion may have been created when it was established that there were human bones buried under the earthworks and ditch.

In any case, Arbor Low certainly must have been a place of special significance. The amount of sustained effort required to bring the stones to that precise location and arrange them in the wheel shape, let alone constructing the earthwork and ditch, must surely indicate that its builders were driven by an immense ritual or social purpose. But what it was remains a mystery.

It is still a centre of religious importance to some. Present day Druids and followers of the Wicca path represent just two of the many religions for whose adherents Arbor Low is a sacred location. Many other people who are interested in the ancient Celtic pagan ways also find their way there,

especially at Belthane, Samhain, Hallowe'en etc. Perhaps if
David and I had returned the next day, May Day, we would
have met people with belief in the magical significance of the
place. It is whispered that a child conceived at Arbor Low
will have occult abilities, though given the cold and windy
location, those involved would need almost superhuman
powers of concentration!

Arbor Low lies at the centre of a network of leylines.
When Alfred Watkins first described the existence of leylines
in his book *The Old Straight Track*, published in 1925,
people were initially quite sceptical. Watkins had noticed
how ancient sites – barrows, stone cairns, burial mounds,
sacred hilltop trees, tumuli – appeared to be aligned. Even
medieval churches seemed to occur in these old straight
lines. This might seem strange as the churches were built
much later than the other sites, but it has to be remembered
that the early Christians – either deliberately or subcon-
sciously – often built churches in places that were already
regarded as sacred.

Once Watkins had pointed out these alignments, others
soon began to discover more of them. At one time it was
suggested that the lines were actually ancient tracks, where
our ancestors had walked from one prominent site to
another, using the tumuli and so on as markers. However,
this theory does raise a few problems. Sometimes the leylines
run across rivers, or over hills, where the natural route
would be for walkers to divert to an easier river crossing
point or to walk around the hill. People soon began to
suggest that leylines might have a more powerful, and less
prosaic, origin. Many leyline hunters are convinced that
these leys follow lines of some ancient natural power, still
not understood by modern science. It is certainly true that
leylines can be detected by dowsers using divining rods, in
the same way that underground streams are discovered. This
power is not magnetism or electricity, but may well be a
natural energy of a similar type: invisible but definitely
present. The energy seems to come from the earth itself, and
to vary in intensity with the seasons.

In Derbyshire many of the place names that end in Low

occur on leylines, and Arbor Low is certainly among the most important. Philip Heselton and Jimmy Goddard, two leading leyline experts, once put forward the theory that England's leylines form a tall isosceles triangle. The base of the triangle runs from Somerset to Essex and the apex – the very top point of the triangle – is at Arbor Low.

An unusually high number of leylines run through the location, though the claim of Paul Screeton, a former editor of the magazine *The Ley Hunter*, that there are 150 of them is usually regarded as excessive. But even if the true number is a third of that figure, it still makes Arbor Low a very important site to students of leylines. In their book *Mysterious Derbyshire*, Philip Rickman and Graham Nown claim that Arbor Low is not only the central powerhouse of Derbyshire, it may be the core of the ley system for the whole of England. They envisage: 'lines of subtle energy flowing from here in fifty or more directions, its passages marked out by stones, mounds, churches and other features. The mounds may be regarded simply as markers or, it has been suggested, as accumulators of the earth power.' These authors suggest that dead bodies may have been placed at Arbor Low in the belief that the power contained within its stones would transport their souls to the afterlife.

One thing is certain. Alfred Watkins did not discover leylines in the 1920s. He rediscovered them, for which we owe him a great debt. The existence of these lines of force – and the existence of the power contained within the sites situated on them – was known to our ancestors thousands of years ago.

Bibliography

Anthony, Wayne, *Haunted Derbyshire*, Breedon Books 1997

Bell, David, *Derbyshire Ghosts & Legends*, Countryside Books 1993

Christian, Roy, *Well-Dressing in Derbyshire*, Derbyshire Countryside Ltd 1987

Clarke, David and Roberts, Andy, *Phantoms of the Sky*, Hale 1990

Clarke, David and Roberts, Andy, *Twilight of the Celtic Gods*, Cassell 1996

Clarke, David, *Supernatural Peak District*, Hale 2000

Collier, Ron and Wilkinson, Roni, *Dark Peak Aircraft Wrecks*, Barnsley Chronicle Group 1979

Daniel, Clarence, *Derbyshire Traditions*, Dalesman Books 1975

Davis, Carol Ann, *Children Who Kill*, Allison & Busby 2003

Garner, Edward, *Hanged for Three Pennies*, Breedon Books 2000

Garner, Edward, *Was You Ever in Dovedale?*, Sigma Leisure 1995

Hale, Don; Huns, Marika and McGregor, Hamish, *Town Without Pity*, Century 2002

Hayward, James, *Myths and Legends of the First World War*, Sutton Publishing 2002

Heselton, Philip, *Leylines*, Hodder & Stoughton 1999

Jones, Keith and Young, John, *Jeremiah Brandreth the Nottingham Captain*, Liberty Tree 1981

Naylor, Peter J, *Celtic Derbyshire*, J H Hall & Sons 1983

Porteous, Crichton, *The Beauty and Mystery of Well-Dressing*, Pilgrim Press Ltd 1949

Pugh, Harry, *Wild Justice: The Lynn Siddons Murder*, Robert Hale 1996

Rickman, Philip and Nown, Graham, *Mysterious Derbyshire*, Dalesman Books 1977

Robinson, Brian, (ed) *The Seven Blunders of the Peak*, Scarthin Books 1994

Rothman, Benny, *The 1932 Kinder Trespass*, Willow Publishing 1982

Sharpe, Neville T, *The Derbyshire Pit Murders*, N T Sharpe 1996